Architectural Hardware

QUARRY

First published in the United States of America by
Quarry Books, a member of
Quayside Publishing Group
33 Commercial Street
Gloucester, Massachusetts 01930-5089
Telephone: (978) 282-9590
Fax: (978) 283-2742
www.rockpub.com

Library of Congress Cataloging-in-Publication Data
Berry, Nancy E.
  Architectural hardware: ideas, inspiration, and practical advice
for adding handles, hinges, knobs, and pulls to your home
    p. cm.
  ISBN 1-59253-295-0 (pbk.)
  1. Finish hardware. 2. Building fittings. I. Title
TH6010.B47 2006
747'.9—DC22   2006012141
                                                    CIP

ISBN-13: 978-1-59253-295-7
ISBN-10: 1-59253-295-0

10 9 8 7 6 5 4 3 2 1

Design: Stephen Gleason Design

Illustrations by: Robert Leanna II

Cover images: Allan Penn; all other photographs by Jonathan Wallen except bottom right image by James Yochum.

Printed in China

HOME DESIGN DETAILS

Architectural Hardware

Ideas, Inspiration, and Practical Advice for Adding Handles,
Hinges, Knobs, and Pulls to Your Home

NANCY E. BERRY

GLOUCESTER MASSACHUSETTS

QUARRY BOOKS

CONTENTS

INTRODUCTION

Several years ago, I found myself the proud owner of my first home—a 1927 Cape Cod–style house.

The house was in remarkably good shape for its years, except for a 1970s master bath addition with green shag carpet and mirrored sliding closet doors—which I had a hard time sliding. I envisioned this space as my sanctuary; a retreat where I could soak in a hot tub surrounded by beautiful fittings. I saw a linen closet with French doors backed in antiqued mirror in a home and garden magazine and thought they would be the perfect replacement for the closet sliders. I worked with a contractor to choose the doors, beveled mirror, and "candle wax" paint color. One item I did not think to specify was the door hardware. When I arrived home from work that day, the contractor had installed the doors but their shiny "brass" doorknobs were cheap dummy knobs that merely snapped into place. After a few months, the knobs became loose and their shiny gold finish started to chip.

I had learned my lesson. Whether taking on a small renovation project or building a new home, it pays to get involved in the design details—right down to the architectural hardware. Hardware not only allows us to navigate the spaces in our homes, but also reflects our home's character. So where does one begin when selecting knobs, latches, hinges, and pulls? The choices in the market today can be mind numbing. There are different styles, price points, grades, and finishes. And what type of hardware is appropriate for what room? In this book, we'll look at the history, form, function, and period styles of hardware, as well as simple how-to projects for replacing outdated hardware. We'll also explore hardware design ideas for a variety of spaces—from a Greek Revival kitchen to an ultramodern bath, to a traditional home office, to an Arts and Crafts entryway. Architect Sandy Vitzthum described architectural hardware this way: "It's a lot like jewelry; you can leave it off, but a woman looks a lot more finished with the appropriate jewelry on."

PART ONE
The Nuts and Bolts

Y ou may not realize it, but architectural hardware is a key element in keeping your home functioning properly. Knobs, hinges, latches, levers, and locks are the working pieces in our homes. Whether it's a hinge that swings a door or a latch that opens a cupboard, these gadgets keep our homes in motion, allowing us to navigate through them. In this section, we'll explore the practical aspects of architectural hardware: the what, why, and how of choosing, finishing, and installing hardware. We'll also discover the history of hardware through the ages and which style of hardware is appropriate for which house design.

A Handle on Hardware

One of the most important elements of house design, and one of the most often overlooked, is the architectural hardware: the knobs, handles, hinges, and levers that allow movement in the home. Wrapped up in the big picture of a renovation or a new construction project, homeowners and contractors alike often forget to consider the small details—including the appropriate hardware that will enhance the mechanics and the aesthetics of the home. Where would we be without these hard-working components? Be it a bolt that secures a door, a pull that slides a drawer, or a crank that opens a window, function must exist along with decoration.

Country of Origin

When shopping for hardware, specifically door hardware, determine in which country the hardware is made. Most European manufacturers make products designed for the American market and vice versa. In fact, a lot of hardware sold in the United States is from Europe. But before purchasing foreign hardware, it is helpful to be aware that certain countries have unique hardware specifications. For instance, France almost strictly uses lever handles for its door and window hardware. The spindles are smooth and ¼" (7 mm) thick, while the English typically produce round and oval doorknobs with spindles that are ⅓" (8 mm) thick. And while in the United States there is a lot of hardware for the do-it-yourselfer, many European countries still consider hardware installation a job best left to a craftsman, so the mechanisms may be a bit more sophisticated. Another point to consider is that most American doors come predrilled with a standard 2⅜" (6.0 cm) diameter to take the hardware. Most French hardware will not have a rose (the metal plate attached to the face of the door around the shaft of the doorknob) that will accommodate this size hole—although the savvy French have come up with an American rose. European and American hinges also differ. Europe typically uses a loose pin hinge while the United States uses the five-knuckle butt hinge. And when Americans talk of hinge size, it is always in inches—as we all know, Europe measures in centimeters! So remember to ask your contractor or hardware manufacturer if the measurement is in inches or centimeters. You may come across a beautiful knob, but if it doesn't fit your door, you'll just have a pretty paperweight.

Casting Call

Another factor to consider when shopping for hardware is how it was made. This can often determine the quality and price. There are three methods used to make hardware: cast, forged, and wrought.

Cast

Sand-casting hardware, made popular in the Victorian era, is still employed today by high-end hardware manufacturers to make marks or pits in the hardware and to give the new hardware the illusion of antiquity. A mold is made by packing sand around a wood model (called a pattern) carved in the design of the final casting. The mold is typically in two parts so the model can be easily removed, leaving a cavity into which the molten metal is poured.

Another method of casting still used today is lost wax casting. An ancient art, lost wax casting affords the most detailed reproduction but is an intricate process. A successful casting starts with shaping a wax pattern—if the pattern isn't finely detailed it won't render a good piece. The wax pattern, or model, is hand chased (tooled) by a skilled artisan to ensure the level of detail. The second step is forming the mold from the pattern by dipping the pattern into a liquid—this material can vary depending on the metal that will be molded (it is typically clay). The combination is placed in a kiln where the wax melts away—or is lost—and only the ceramic mold remains. This mold is then filled with molten metal to produce the hardware.

Pressed casting is a process in which the metal is pressed or stamped with a pattern. This method typically doesn't create fine detailing and is fairly inexpensive. In the late 1800s, many pieces were produced this way and today some companies still employ this technique.

Forged and Wrought

Forged hardware is the process of hammering or rolling metal into shape and is the method used by early blacksmiths. The term is also used to describe modern mass production. Forging produces high-quality hardware but typically cannot capture the intricate designs found on decorative pieces. "Wrought" means that metal is rolled into flat strips, and then punched or die-cut, which can produce any thickness of hardware—from a thin back plate (a doorknob escutcheon usually larger than a rose), to a thick hinge. Die-cut pieces are less expensive than cast pieces.

Above: Different methods of casting can affect the look of the hardware. This handsome reproduction hardware was cast to produce a smooth handle.

Right: This elaborate decorative lever is an example of the detail the lost wax casting method can produce.

Door Hardware

Changing door hardware is a popular do-it-yourself project for homeowners, but before you purchase new locks or hinges, get to know your home's door hardware argot, or the "hand" of the door. The hand refers to the swing of the door. If the hinges are on the left side of the door as you walk through, it is a left-handed door. If the hinges are on the right, it is a right-handed door.

Carefully measure the hardware and its openings when replacing older components. For instance, before replacing a doorknob, examine the spindle. Most exterior doorknobs have spindles that are ⅜" (1 cm) thick while interior doors spindles are ⁵⁄₁₆" (8 mm) thick. Antique spindles are smooth and secure the knob with side-set screws. These older knobs also have washers that hold the knobs securely to the rose. Newer knobs have threaded spindles. There are several standard spindles for knobs, so don't assume that every knob will fit every door. Also note the orientation of the spindle when the lock is in place. Is the spindle on the diamond or on the square? If a knob's hole is shaped like a diamond, the spindle is said to be "on the diamond." European knobs are placed on the square, while American knobs are placed on the diamond. The wrong orientation will leave an oval or lever handle at an odd angle. Once you have determined the door standards, make sure those standards match those of the hardware you are considering. If purchasing a new lever handle for an old lock, check that the lock can carry the weight of the lever. If the internal springs are too weak to lift the lever, the lock won't operate.

Hand of a Door

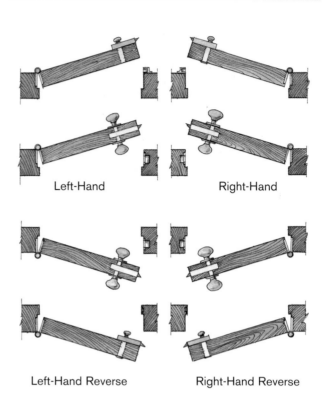

Left-Hand   Right-Hand

Left-Hand Reverse   Right-Hand Reverse

Trade Tip

Another factor to consider when selecting door hardware is your insurance rates. Insurance companies are investing a significant amount of money and resources toward increasing the stringency and rigor of codes, and design pressure (DP) testing is also becoming an industry standard.

Mortise Lockset and Hinge

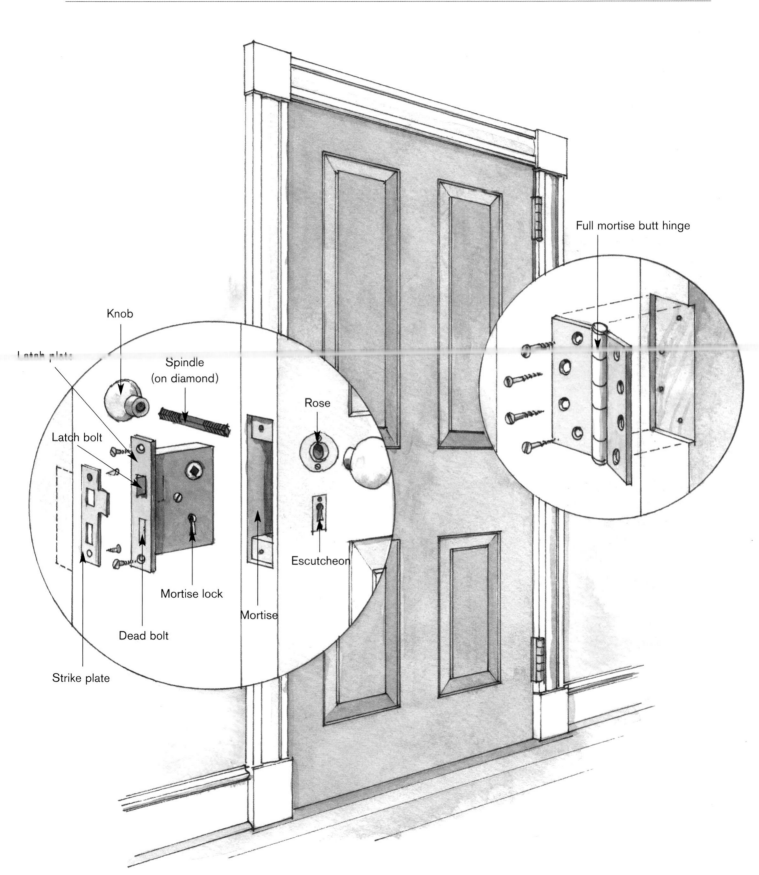

Full mortise butt hinge

Knob

Spindle
(on diamond)

Latch plate

Latch bolt

Strike plate

Dead bolt

Mortise lock

Mortise

Rose

Escutcheon

Locks

Growing up in a household of ten, I can clearly remember my parents' last instructions as they rushed out the door to work in the morning: "The last one to leave, lock up!" Locks offer security and piece of mind when it comes to protecting the ones you love as well as all your most prized possessions—whether it's the plasma television or the heirloom silver. The technology of residential locks has advanced over the years to include such mechanisms as keyless entry (popular in hotels), where you type a code into a keypad and, voila, the door is unlocked. (I personally like the feel of the key in my hand as I enter my home.)

When purchasing a lockset for your exterior doors, consider the grade of lock you are purchasing. If your locks don't make the grade, your safety and security could be compromised. The two most popular locksets for the home today are the mortise lock and the cylindrical lock. But remember, each country has its own devices for locks, so if you are specifying hardware from overseas, make sure it is compatible with the size and style of your doors.

Rim locks, typically imported from England, were used throughout Colonial America until the mortise lock was invented in the late 1700s. Today, the rim lock has been reintroduced into traditional residential designs.

Grading Locks

When purchasing a lock, check what grade is accepted by your building codes. The American National Standards Institute (ASNI) in the United States and the International Organization for Standardization in Europe develop and maintain standards that comparatively measure the security, strength, durability, finish, and performance of locks. The American standard grades locks as one, two, or three, with one being the best. The grades represent the minimum torque the knob will resist before failing, which ranges from 120 inches per pound for grade three, to 150 inches per pound for grade two, to 300 inches per pound for grade one. Levers are tested at higher standards. Longevity tests require grade-three locks to cycle 200 times; that equates to operating the door ten times a day for 54 years. Grade-two locks test at 400,000 cycles, and grade one at 800,000.

Latch and Strike

The latch mechanism throws the bolt when the knob or lever is turned. There are three types of latches:

SPRING: typically a ½" (1.3 cm) beveled latch for interior doors

DEADLOCKING: a ½" (1.3 cm) beveled latch with a deadlocking bar, that needs a key push button to lock or unlock

DEADBOLT: a 1" (2.5 cm) through bolt that locks into position with a key

Mortise Locks

If a home was built before 1940, chances are it will have mortise locks and latches. Invented in England around 1790, mortise locks are boxes mounted in deep, square recesses chiseled into a door edge. The lock is operated by notches on the key, which engage with levers in the lock. Mortise locks have been mass-produced for more than 150 years. Although found on both exterior and interior doors, today, they are often reserved for exterior and high-end interior doors. They're heavy and durable, and older ones are worth keeping. Some common problems, such as weak latch tension, are typically due to worn-out pins or springs. If you have old mortise locks, work with an experienced locksmith to determine whether he can get the piece functioning smoothly again. If you need to replace the existing mortise lock, make sure you purchase one with the same dimensions as the old one. If you're incorporating a mortise lock on a new door, the door needs to be at least 1¼" (3 cm) thick in order to accomodate a mortise lock. The most common size mortise lock is 4" (10.7 cm) deep.

The mortise lock largely replaced the rim lock, a box mounted to the exterior of the door. A handsome fixture, many high-end hardware-manufacturing companies are reproducing eighteenth-century rim locks for entry doors today.

Trade Tip

- Tubular locks are more expensive than cylinder locks

- Tubular locks can fit almost any door by adjusting the spindle

- Cylindrical locks are sturdier than a tubular lock

- Cylindrical locks distribute loads on the latch more evenly

Mortise locks are most commonly used on exterior doors or on high-end interior doors.

Cylinder and Tubular Locks

If a house was built after 1940, it will most likely have cylinder or tubular locks. Both designs are bored-in locksets, named for the installation in which a hole is bored through the door. In 1848, Linus Yale, Jr. invented a domestic lock—better known today as the cylinder lock—a modification of an ancient Egyptian design that used a pin tumbler. A cylinder lock easily mounts into a round hole cut into the door. Because installation is so easy, they have usurped mortise locks in many residential applications. In the 1920s, Walter Schlage advanced the concept of a cylindrical pin-tumbler lock by placing a push-button locking mechanism between two knobs. Emphasis was on security yet, equally important, the lock became an intricate part of the door design with only the fittings showing.

Today, tubular locks are inexpensive and typically not as sturdy as a cylindrical lock. (Some manufacturers do make good quality tubular locks.) The advantage to using a tubular lock is that you can fit it to any door thickness by adjusting the spindle. A tubular lock typically has a square spindle that runs from knob to knob, which passes through a spring-loaded latch installed through the door's edge. Cylindrical locks have more functions than tubular locks. Their mechanism distributes loads on the latch more evenly than in tubular locks. Cylindrical locks have independent spindles that are attached to the knobs. The spindles overlap in the center of the door and activate a spring-loaded latch bolt from the end of the latch assembly. Ratings for locksets are not mandatory, and many hardware manufacturers do not send their hardware to be rated although the quality may be superior.

Right: These nineteenth-century reproduction cobalt blue knobs add a graceful touch to the faux-grained salon doors.

Lock History

As a mechanical device that secures a door, gate, or cabinet, locks have been around since ancient times. In fact, locks are mentioned throughout the Old Testament. The oldest known recorded use of locks was in 4,000 BC in Egypt.

The oldest discovered lock is from Khorsabad Palace in Persia and dates from 720 BC. Made with a set of wooden pins inside a wooden staple, the pins drop into a set of matching holes in the bolt. A wooden bar was used as the key. (Today's cylinder lock and key works on this same principle.)

We know that around 300 BC, the Greeks used a bolt lock in which the bolt could be lifted through an opening by a sickle type key. The Romans used locks that were more ornate and complex. One type of Roman key had a ring attached to it so it could be worn on the finger. The oldest discovered metal lock dates from about 870 AD and appeared in England. In the eighteenth century, the English became leaders in lock making, studying ancient Roman locks as well as French and German designs. And by the 1840s, English lock makers developed the pickproof lock. Between 1774 and 1920, American lock makers patented some 3,000 varieties of locks.

Above: Cylinder locks are a bit sturdier than tubular locks and are standard in new construction today.

Knobs

Ubiquitous devices in homes today, round and oval knobs come in a variety of materials. In fact, it would not be unusual for a small house, only 2,000 square feet (186 sq m) in size, to have as many as 50 knobs! And before you go shopping, it's best to know which type of knob you will need for which door. Depending on how the lockset will be used in your home, there are four types of knobs for your interiors to consider. For hallways and closets, passage knobs are popular because they have no locking mechanism. Privacy locksets are used on bathroom or bedroom doors and are locked from the inside with a push button on the center of the knob or the rose. If security or safety is an issue, say for an attic or basement door, keyed locksets are preferred. A dummy knob is a knob screwed to the door but that doesn't have any internal working parts; it is typically used with a roller catch to secure the door. Dummy knobs are often used on closet or double doors, for instance, with a pair of French doors—one door would contain a working latch while the other had a dummy.

Blacksmiths forged the earliest examples of knobs, but by the mid-1600s, some knobs were filed and finished by whitesmiths into polished and decorative forms. In the mid-1800s, inexpensive, brown clay or pottery knobs became common in simple farmhouses as were inexpensive wood knobs. Cast iron, though affordable and durable, was never in fashion. In the early 1800s, highly decorative and expensive free-blown glass knobs were popular in grand houses. By 1836, sockets and ferrules allowed glass knobs to turn in a conventional manner. Today, some of the most common knobs, both antique and reproduction, are cast or die-cut in brass and bronze.

William K. Vanderbilt

In 1892, William K. Vanderbilt built the opulent Marble House in Newport, Rhode Island, for his wife Alva and requested that the doors throughout the mansion be installed without knobs. He employed footmen to open the doors from inside rooms so his guests would never be troubled with operating a doorknob—the ultimate in luxury. This Golden Age gesture of wealth and opulence was as unpractical then as it is now and, needless to say, didn't catch on as a trend.

Levers vs. Knobs

LEVERS are often compliant with Americans with Disabilities Act Regulations.

KNOBS take more wrist motion to turn.

LEVERS are handed; **KNOBS** are not.

LEVERS are gaining popularity in the housing industry.

This oval-shaped knob with a floral design is a reproduction of a nineteenth-century design.

Latches

Latches make up the oldest group of door hardware and are typically operated by pressing a lever with the thumb, hence the term thumb latch. Early thumb latches were made of wood and string, then of wrought iron until they became virtually obsolete in the 1800s with the invention of the rim lock. The latch mechanism was reintroduced at the 1876 World's Fair. Cast in decorative brass and bronze and paired with a back plate and lock, the latch is a familiar welcome for many homeowners. Today, the thumb latch is popular for entryway door sets although the mechanism is far more sophisticated than the earliest designs.

The inside latch lifts to release the door when pressed by the thumb.

Levers

Levers are horizontal handles that originated in Europe. Unlike knobs, levers are handed and will only work properly if placed on either the right- or left-hand side of the door. As with hinges, this is an important point to remember when ordering lever handles. For the elderly or disabled, selecting hardware that is easy to operate is an important consideration; lever handles and minimum clearances between hardware and adjacent walls are the answer.

Many designers are beginning to specify levers for their projects because their superior ergonomics comply with the Americans with Disabilities Act (ADA) regulations.

This lever handle is made of stainless steel.

Trade Tip

There are different knobs for different functions in your home: A **dummy knob** has no internal working parts and is best used on closet doors. A **passage knob** has no locking mechanism and is suitable for hallways. A **privacy lockset** is locked from the inside and used on bedroom and bathroom doors. A **keyed lockset** is secured with a key often used on basement doors.

A traditional solid, turned-brass lever

Ergonomics

The Americans with Disabilities Act (ADA) is national legislation that specifies the handicapped accessibility standards to be used in most buildings, whether public or private facilities. These requirements have been widely adopted. Individual states may have additional codes that overlap ADA. All of these codes reference door hardware. Today, most European countries have their own set of codes, but the European Union (EU) is working to create standardized codes for its member countries.

Egress Codes

The American Society for Testing and Materials (ASTM) has a grading system for security ratings for doors and hardware (on a scale of 10 to 40) using impact tests. These grading systems are being used more frequently in areas subject to hurricanes and high winds. Doors need to be engineered correctly to withstand most of these tests. The lock mechanism helps but it cannot compensate for a weakness in the door itself. Codes vary from country to country, region to region, and from town to town. For instance, weather bands, based on weather studies within the state, influence Florida's building codes. Where wind forces are strongest, stricter codes are enforced. When installing new locksets on your doors, check with your local township for residential building codes.

Working with a Designer

Design options for hardware have increased tremendously over the years. And to meet the conflicting requirements of the public and private realms, the complexity of hardware functions and technologies has also been evolving. When it comes to choosing hardware for your home, be sure your designer or architect is up to speed on the latest codes and technologies.

Quality Control

Sturdy latches, heavy castings, stronger return springs, and better-fitting parts make higher quality locksets but also make the hardware more expensive. Many companies use a sand-cast process that produces new hardware that looks worn and pitted—giving it an Old World effect. The method of casting and finish demands a higher price but has little to do with how a piece actually operates.

Blacksmith shops are reproducing Old World–style strap hinges for new construction projects. Note the number and length of the hinges used to hold up this wide Dutch door.

Hinges

Hinges give doors the ability to swing and, like levers, are handed. Hinges also carry the weight of a door so it is important to know the hinge's load-bearing capacity, which the hinge manufacturer will be able to supply. If economy is a factor when purchasing door hardware, put your money into the hinges—a weak hinge can warp a door.

Hinges can be divided into two general types: straps and butts. The oldest type, the strap hinge, is placed on the face or surface of the door, while the butt hinge is mortised into the butt edge of the door and the door-frame. Strap hinges come in a variety of lengths from 3" to 16" (7.6 to 40.6 cm) long. Variations of the strap hinge are the T-, H-, or HL-hinges—named for the letter shape they emulate. (T-hinges are used when the width of the jamb is restricted.)

Butt hinges also come in a variety of forms. A standard interior or passage door hinge is the five-knuckle butt that typically has the pin fastened in place. The highest-grade butts are cast bronze or brass. Another popular hinge is the loose joint butt; a door hung on this type of hinge can be easily lifted off. The pin in a loose pin butt can be taken out to unhinge the door. This type of hinge is reversible; its advantage is its increased load-bearing surface. Also, because the pin is distinct from the leaves of the hinge, it can be made of a metal that will withstand more wear than the bronze or iron butts.

Trade Tip

Hollow core doors need only two hinges because they are fairly light, while solid core doors need three hinges because they are heavy.

Butterfly Hinge

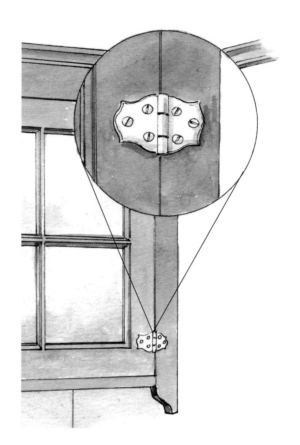

A butt hinge with its pin topped with a finial is a common type of hinge.

Parliament Hinges

When a door is required to open up to 180 degrees it usually needs to clear a projection such as the door-frame's molding. In this situation, parliament hinges can be used. The screw holes on these hinges are aligned along the edge of the hinge flap so the knuckle projects beyond the edge of the door. The further the projection of the knuckle, the greater the angle of opening.

Manufactured since the early 1800s, the olive knuckle hinge is named for its shape. Conventional olive knuckle hinges operate on a pivot shaft inserted into a bore in the knuckle with a bearing ring between the two knuckles. Because the weight of the door is not in line with the pivot, the bores and the bearing ring can quickly wear if the hinge isn't of good quality.

Harmon Hinge

Named for its English inventor, the Harmon hinge is a recessed or pocket pivot hinge. This hinge is perfect for tight spaces because no part of the hinge projects beyond the face of a door when it is either open or closed—the door swings clear of its opening and folds back at a right angle to its closed position. The door can also open into a pocket to form a deep, paneled reveal.

Invented in England, the olive knuckle hinge is a handsome alternative for doors and cabinets.

Window Hardware

Do your windows keep you up at night, shaking and rattling at the slightest bit of wind? It could be that your window fasteners are no longer working properly. The two most common residential windows are casement and double hung. Here's what you need to know about buying new locks for your old windows or old window locks for your new windows.

Double-Hung Window

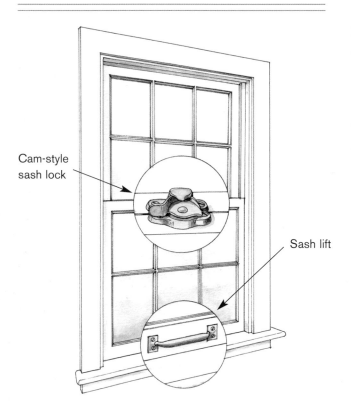

Cam-style sash lock

Sash lift

Trade Tip

When specifying hardware for windows, check the measurements of the sash for the appropriate sash lock, strike, and lift size.

Double Hung

A double-hung window—a window that has two vertically sliding sashes—is a common window type in the United States. The most common types of double-hung window hardware are fasteners and sash lifts. Fasteners help secure a window from intruders as well as prevent air leaks and rattles. To achieve the latter two functions, the window sash should sit snugly against the window frame. The most common sash fasteners are cam (crescent-shaped) locks. There are several styles offered in the marketplace—from Eastlake to ultramodern. When specifying hardware for windows, check details for the appropriate sash lock as well as lift size.

By the Victorian era, sash lifts were common fixtures on windows and are still in use today. Flush, handle, and hook lifts in the appropriate shape and color can add a finishing touch to your sash. If you're looking to add a more detailed look to off-the-shelf double hung windows or if you have old wood windows with loose, rusted, or inoperable hardware, it's a good time to shop for replacements.

Above: The cam-style sash lock paired with sash lifts is a ubiquitous fixture on many windows both old and new.

Right: This dining room is flooded with natural light through these sash windows with crescent cam locks.

Casements

Casement windows with leaded glass panes were the most common domestic window until the mid-1600s, when sash windows were introduced. Sash windows are typically used in Great Britain and the United States, while casement windows are still used in Europe. The casement window swings open on a hinged sash. Architects such as Frank Lloyd Wright reintroduced casement windows in the early 1900s (Wright used horizontal bands of casement windows). Architects specializing in Tudor and Spanish Revival houses of the 1920s and 1940s also introduced the casement window into their designs. There are a number of fasteners and adjusters on the market today—some popular styles resemble medieval designs for use on Tudor and Arts and Crafts Revival houses. Casement fasteners play the same role as double-hung sash fasteners—to secure the window—while casement adjusters hold the window open. The casement, which opens out, and the awning window, which opens up, are still the most popular types of windows in Europe and are gaining popularity in the United States.

Casement Window Hardware

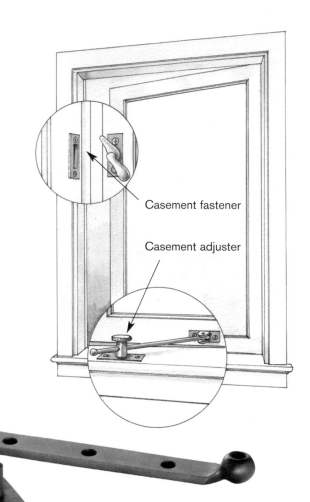

Casement fastener

Casement adjuster

Above: A casement adjuster holds the window open.

Trade Tip

When specifying hardware for awning and casement windows, make sure you look at all your options. For instance, the three-point European lock is a popular choice today.

Right: Popular in contemporary homes today, iron casement fasteners contrast against the stark white window trim.

Left: Traditionally styled casement fasteners come in an assortment of finishes, including antique brass.

Cabinet Hardware

Cabinet hardware offers an inexpensive way to add personality to your decor. The most common types of cabinet and drawer hardware are knobs, drawer pulls, handles, and cupboard catches. Knobs and pulls can be used with either furniture or cabinetry and there are no rules for their placement. You can think of them as both artistic accents and functional pieces. One key difference between them is that knobs are installed with a single screw while pulls are installed with two screws. If you are replacing a pull, remember to measure from the center to the center of each screw to determine the size pull you need for an identical replacement. However, if you are patching the holes or using a back plate, you will increase your options.

Through the centuries, notable cabinetmakers such as Thomas Chippendale and George Hepplewhite enhanced their exquisite furniture with hardware. The Chinese-influenced Chippendale period (1750 to 1785) featured large, heavy brasses in bat wing shapes. Hepplewhite (1785 to 1815) featured stamped brass oval pulls with back plates of concentric circles. Other periods for cabinet hardware include: the William and Mary period (1690 to 1720) featuring cotter pin–attached cast-brass teardrop pulls on dressers; the Queen Anne period (1720 to 1750), showcasing engraved brass back plates with narrow bail (half circle) pulls; Sheraton pulls (1785 to 1815), featuring round back plates and round bail pulls; and the American Empire period, during which animal motifs such as lion heads were popular. The Victorian era, 1860 to 1910, featured teardrop pulls and highly decorative stamped brass pieces, porcelain knobs, and wood knobs as well as built-in pantry and kitchen cabinets with bronze and brass crescent pulls, cupboard catches, and simple knobs.

When replacing hardware, be sure it will be sturdy enough to actually function. And remember to use slotted screws if you desire a period look—Phillips head screws are a 1940s invention. Knobs and pulls don't have to be of the same style but their finishes should be compatible with the other hardware in the room (and remember that they also need to harmonize with any exposed hinges).

Trade Tip

Generally, a single knob or pull is used on drawers under 18" (45.7 cm) wide, while drawers wider than 18" (45.7 cm) use either two knobs or two pulls.

Decorative Victorian drop pulls add visual interest to a simple dresser. When replacing drawer pulls, make sure the pull can take the weight of the drawer as well as its contents.

Exterior Hardware

Just as interior knobs, pulls, and hinges can add style and personality to your home, the right architectural hardware on the exterior of your home can make it both functional and fantastic. Here are a few areas to consider adding sparkle, flair, and functionality to your home.

Screen Door Hardware

Remember the wonderful snap of your grandmother's screen door when you were a kid? Traditional wood screen doors are making a comeback and have their own types of catches and hinges that make them work smoothly. Spring-loaded hinges allow a light screen door to close securely, keeping insects out of the house. There are a few companies that make reproduction offset hinges for antique screen doors that fit loosely into the jamb.

Hinges are always screwed to the screen door on the same side as the primary door. Screen door latch sets come in rim, tubular, mortise, and push-pull. Screen doors have thinner frames than primary doors so a latch bolt is typically $5/8$" (1.6 cm) thick. When positioning your screen door hardware, be sure it does not interfere with your primary door's hardware. It's best to stagger the height of the primary door handle and the screen door handle so they don't collide. If the screen door is left natural, use brass or galvanized hinges.

Trade Tip

When installing your screen door hardware, be sure that it does not interfere with your primary door's hardware.

Antique screen door hardware in good shape is hard to come by. Many manufacturers are replicating antique screen door hardware for homes today.

Screen Door Hardware

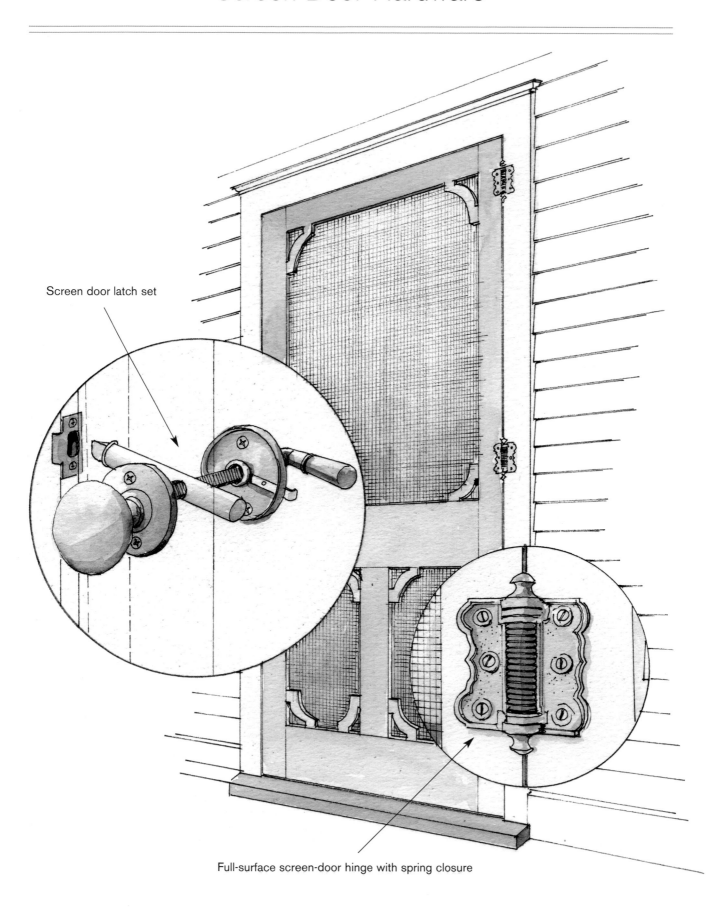

Screen door latch set

Full-surface screen-door hinge with spring closure

Accessories

If you've ever strolled down a Paris street, such as the rue de Rivoli, you will be familiar with the bright blue plates with white house numbers stamped on the entryways of buildings—a quintessential Parisian hardware accessory. Mailboxes, mail slots, radiator covers, switch plates, as well as house numbers all fall under the category of architectural hardware. When choosing the accessories for the exterior of your home, such as a doorknocker and house numbers, finish the pieces in the same colors and materials. The finish will tie the interior design together, as well. For instance, if you are decorating a room and have antiqued brass doorknobs, finish your switch plates in the same antiqued brass.

A decorative brass door knocker from the eighteenth century.

Shutters

Shutter hardware comes in a variety of shapes and sizes, so it's important to understand how the shutters function in order to properly mount them. Second-floor shutters are sometimes louvered to let in night breezes, while solid shutters give added security to first-floor rooms. All shutters require some type of hinge to allow movement and a hook or shutter dog to hold the shutter open. Operable shutters are hinged to the outside edge of the window close to the window recess. A common hinge type of the past was the strap-and-pintle, where the metal strap pivots on an upright pin. The Lull and Porter hinge allows a shutter to lock into an open or closed position. Strap hinges are also popular because they help support the shutter. Shutter dogs come in a variety of shapes—S, rattail, and long arm are a few common forms.

Shutters come in a variety of shapes and sizes and so does shutter hardware. When choosing shutter hardware for your home, make sure you use appropriate finishes and styles.

CHAPTER Two

Hinging on the Past

Whatever style house you have, there is period-inspired hardware on the market that will suit your taste—whether an original 1880s doggie doorknob from P. & F. Corbin or Euro-style pulls for your super sleek kitchen. Several companies are selling or recasting historically accurate designs for old or historically inspired houses, so when it comes to fitting out doors, windows, and built-ins with hardware, your choices are vast and varied.

Preindustrial Revolution

Before the 1800s, function, not fashion, dictated the design of architectural hardware. Hand-forged iron hinges, latches, and heavy rim locks offered utility without much flair for the wooden saltbox houses of colonial America and Europe. Pre-1700 houses were built strictly for practicality, not curb appeal. The hallmarks of this historic house design are its box-shaped plan, heavy timber frame, wood shingle or clapboard façade, a steep pitch gabled roof, and center chimney. Twelve-over-twelve or nine-over-nine windows and board-and-batten front doors topped with transoms were also standard features. Local blacksmiths forged strap hinges and thumb latches of imported English iron for these early post-medieval structures. The most common door

hardware design was the Suffolk bean latch, named for the handle plate and the region in England where it originated. Blacksmiths varied the design by forging hearts, spears, and tulip shapes for the handle plate. Heavy strap, H-, and HL-hinges supported these early doors.

With the advent of better building techniques in the early 1700s, the elegant Georgian style was introduced with all its decorative curved lines and flourishes. The grandest Georgian homes had brass hardware made in brass works in Birmingham, England. After 1776, the Federal style took hold in America when the dressiest a knob might have gotten was a cloak of silver soldered or sweated onto brass. The Greek Revival style appeared in the 1820s and found its way not only into southern plantation homes—think Scarlet O'Hara's Tara—but also into small farmhouses and city town houses. Introduced in the early 1800s, pressed glass knobs began to dress interior doors in such popular colors as blue and amethyst, or transparent uncolored glass. American inventor Enoch Robinson (1801 to 1888), who patented a glass-pressing machine, produced some of the finest examples of glass knobs in the United States from 1836 until his death.

Another ubiquitous knob in this era was the mineral knob; an inexpensive alternative to glass, the mineral knob came in jet, porcelain, and brown.

During the Colonial era, simple wrought iron thumb latches were used on farmhouse doors.

Victorian: 1860 to 1910

Architectural hardware blossomed in the late 1800s in both America and Europe. The Industrial Revolution, new house designs, and Victorian artistic sensibilities gave rise to a decorative hardware makeover. Innovative casting methods enabled companies to mass-produce hardware at affordable prices. With this new sand-cast technology, they could create hundreds of pieces a day as compared to hand forging, which could only produce a dozen or so in the same time.

Along with advances in production came changes in fashion and attitudes. Tastes had shifted from the conservative to the elaborate for every aspect of the home, and architectural hardware was no exception. Bold Queen Anne, Italianate, and Second Empire house styles began popping up in the new suburbia, which needed hardware to complement their architecture. The concept of extending a building's general design into its details and fittings was fairly new at the time. Following this philosophy, many renowned architects began designing suites of hardware for their own buildings. Among them was Louis Sullivan, who designed hardware for his architectural masterpieces.

In 1869 in the United States, the Metallic Compression Casting Company, a small Connecticut firm, was awarded its first design patents for decorative hardware; by 1870, the company offered a full portfolio of decorative knobs. This innovation sparked several large hardware manufacturers such as P. & F. Corbin, Yale and Towne, and Russell and Erwin to follow suit.

By 1872, Russell and Erwin had hired a "trained designer" to create fanciful patterns for its business.

The ornamental inspiration for hardware designs came from every corner of the globe and from every historical period. The Byzantine Empire, Colonial America, sixteenth-century England, Amsterdam, ancient Egypt, and China were just a few periods and places tapped for their aesthetic sensibilities. Yale and Towne divided its hardware design categories into twenty four schools and each school could have as many as fifty different decorative patterns. Names such as Lilbourn, Adams, Stratford, Brabant, and Osaka reflected the design motif on the metal. In 1858, Japan opened up trade to the world after 250 years of isolation, which led to many Japanese motifs and symbols—Geisha girls, bamboo shoots, and chrysanthemums—being transferred onto knobs and hinges.

During the Victorian era, England's tastemakers made a splash in both America and Europe. One well-respected talent was Christopher Dresser, today regarded as the first industrial designer. A pupil of Owen Jones (author of *The Grammar of Ornament*), Dresser designed hardware patterns for a host of Birmingham, England, foundries and copies of his work soon appeared in America. Another well-known Victorian-era tastemaker, Charles Locke Eastlake, wrote *Hints on Household Taste* in 1868, which was a smash hit in the United States, although Americans hungry for ornament often misinterpreted Eastlake's message. Eastlake, who was fighting against the Industrial Revolution's cheap factory-made goods, wanted his readers to embrace handcrafts, but his readership missed the point entirely. Instead, houses were decked out in fanciful mass-produced hardware.

In Victorian times, not only did knobs receive decorative details but the rosettes did as well.

Colonial– and Spanish–Revival Styles; Romantic: 1880s to 1940s

At the end of the nineteenth century, housing styles changed yet again. The United States, Britain, and France were looking back to the past to revive historical house types. The United States had recently celebrated its centennial, breeding nostalgia for its past. Americans yearned for the simpler times of the colonial era. Well-known Boston architect Robert Peabody of Peabody and Stearns asked in an article, "With our centennial year, have we not discovered that we have a past worthy of study?" An emphasis on hearth and home was at the center of the Colonial Revival aesthetic.

Architectural firm McKim, Mead and White is best known for Colonial Revival houses—particularly its interiors. The style was based on "innovative adaptation" and "historical recall." Colonial Revival hardware was typically simple brass pieces—replications of imported pieces from seventeenth-century England. In England, architects looked to the quaint stone houses of the past to create the Cotswold cottage, also called the Hansel and Gretel cottage. In Germany, the Bavarian chalet was reinvented for the new century.

In addition to colonial America, architects, house builders, and house kit purveyors also looked to English Tudor, Spanish, and French Norman styles for ideas. Houses inspired by these past forms sprung up through the early decades of the twentieth century. And the revival hardware for these homes was rustic, charming, and made of iron. This type of hardware was mass-produced but gave the appearance—from a distance—of being hand forged. Because of its medieval origins, the hardware designs were interchangeable from one house style to another. An iron door knocker was advertised as being appropriate for either a Spanish Colonial or French Norman villa, or for an Arts and Crafts bungalow.

Preindustrial

If you have a home built before 1860 or have a Colonial-inspired home, these are some hardware styles to add:

KNOBS: brass, porcelain, cut and blown glass

LATCHES: wrought iron

HINGES: wrought-iron strap, H, and HL

Cabinet hardware: wooden knobs, button turns, bail pulls

Victorian–Inspired

If your home was built between 1860 and 1910 or was inspired by the Victorian style, consider adding:

KNOBS: decorative brass, bronze, cast iron

HINGES: decorative butt, olive knuckle

CABINET HARDWARE: cast iron, brass, nickel-plated cupboard catches, bin pulls

Revival–Inspired

If you have an authentic Revival home or a Revival-inspired home, you should look to incorporate:

KNOBS: brass with medieval motifs, glass

LEVERS: handled iron, brass, medieval motifs

HINGES: iron and brass strap hinges (often decorative)

CABINET HARDWARE: iron and hand hammered pulls

Shown is a lever-handle lockset and ornamental studs that cover it. The 1920s represented the century's height of decorative blacksmithing; a piece of hardware that couldn't be obtained in the extensive catalogs of the day, such as this one, could be readily custom fabricated.

Arts and Crafts: 1900s to 1930s

By 1900, progressive architects and designers were moving away from the superfluous machine-cut details of the Victorian era to simpler, more practical, and less historical house designs. Influenced by the Arts and Crafts movement and its noted leaders, including America's Gustav Stickley and England's William Morris, architects began designing low, horizontal buildings with overhanging eaves and deep porches. Spatial continuity between home and garden was central to the Arts and Crafts philosophy. This philosophy inspired architects to find new ways to bridge interior and exterior spaces, with the entryway being the obvious place to start. Morris challenged Victorian society to "Have nothing in your homes that you do not know to be useful, or believe to be beautiful." And this philosophy reached right down to the doorknob.

Doors

Medieval in appearance and proportions, yet modern in construction, the Arts and Crafts door became a key element in the new wave of bungalows, Foursquares, and Craftsman-style houses popping up across the country at the turn of the twentieth century. Carrying the idea of unified house design to the functional components, the Arts and Crafts door approached a level of artwork. The doors that designers chose for these house types were often wider than conventional doors, sometimes 12" (30.5 cm) wider than the standard 36" (91.4 cm). Their horizontality and breadth were enhanced by sidelights accented with geometric designs.

Aside from their proportions, the doors adopted a rustic, hand-hewn, hand-finished appearance—whether they were constructed by hand or not. Custom doors would often feature oversized wrought iron hinge straps, playing up the medieval feel. Typically unpainted, like the Arts and Crafts interior woodwork, the doors were stained

Arts and Crafts–Inspired

If you have an authentic or Arts and Crafts–inspired home:

KNOBS: brass, copper, nature motifs

HINGES: brass, iron, heavy strap hinges

CABINET HARDWARE: wood, brass, geometric forms

Art Deco–Inspired

If you have an authentic or Art Deco–Inspired home:

KNOBS: brass, streamlined, ziggurat shapes

HINGES: butt hinges, surface-mounted hinges

CABINET HARDWARE: Bakelite, Lucite, brass

Taking inspiration from the Arts and Crafts vocabulary, the designer of this door hardware pulls out all the stops. Its great impact lies in the extraordinary set of matching brass hardware with a stylized oak leaf and acorn motif.

or clear finished to capitalize on the beauty of the oak or cedar used, with the striking antiqued hardware adding a visual element. Door patterns in the Arts and Crafts houses tended toward rectilinear shapes with bold motifs. Visual appeal came from structural details such as the pronounced stiles and rails of the doorframe, hand-wrought hardware and hinges, and exposed joinery in contrast to the applied decoration of the Victorian era.

Principles

Arts and Crafts hardware draws on preindustrial metals such as bronze, brass, copper, and iron, while rough surfaces simulate hand hammering or ancient casting. Designs may also consist of rectilinear grids and geometrical shapes. Some architects of the era designed the house and all its components, including the hardware. British designers C.F.A. Voysey and Charles Rennie Mackintosh designed cabinet hinges and doorknockers along with the molding and mantels in their house designs. Frank Lloyd Wright was notorious for his fastidious attention to detail and designed suites of hardware for his houses. American architects Charles and Henry Greene carried their design aesthetic into the service areas of the house, including the kitchen's elongated wooden drawer pulls. Although this approach worked wonderfully for wealthy clients, most of the housing stock was not of such pedigree that supplying hardware for these houses required mass production. In 1902, American designer Gustav Stickley began to produce a hardware line for his popular furniture designs made in his Craftsman Workshops. Stickley's catalogs offered iron, brass, and copper hardware finished with hand-applied patina and hand hammering.

He wrote in his catalog, "None of the glittering, fragile metal then in vogue was possible in conjunction with [the furniture's] straight severe lines and plain surfaces. So I opened a metal-work department in the Craftsman Workshops, and there we made plain, strong handles, pulls, hinges, and escutcheons of iron, copper, and brass, so designed and made that each article fulfilled as simply and directly as possible the purpose for which it was intended, and so finished that the natural beauty of each metal was shown as frankly as was the quality of the wood against which it was placed."

Many other hardware manufacturers followed suit and produced not just Arts and Crafts hardware but medieval pieces that could be applied to Colonial and Spanish Revival, bungalow, and Tudor houses.

Trade Tip

• The borehole on an antique door is much smaller than today's borehole.

• When fitting an antique knob on a new, predrilled door, order a reproduction rosette that will fit over the hole.

• The Old Rose Company manufactures reproduction designs in modern proportions. (See Resources, page 170).

Original Gustav Stickley cabinet pulls dress the front of this built-in sideboard in a California bungalow.

Art Deco: 1920s to 1930s

Actress Jean Harlow was often featured on screen lounging in glamorous boudoirs in her 1920s and 1930s films such as Blonde Bombshell or Dinner at Eight. These sleek movie sets reflected a new movement in design known today as Art Deco. The Art Deco style movement got its start in France. At the 1925 *Exposition International des Arts Decoratifs et Industriels Modernes* held in Paris, all past design vocabularies were excluded from the exhibition and only the most modern designers with an eye toward the future were allowed to exhibit. Designers influenced by cubism and futurism employed stepped forms such as the ziggurat and rounded corners in geometric order. The style was quickly introduced to the United States, first at the Metropolitan Museum of Art in 1926, and soon found its way into the modern skyscrapers and high-rise apartments of the era, particularly in New York and Miami. The Empire State Building (1930) and Chrysler Building (1930) are examples of Art Deco–influenced designs. In these commercial buildings, Art Deco found expression in all aspects of the interior ornamentation—including the hardware. Streamlined styles reminiscent of airplanes and ocean liners showed up on door levers and drawer pulls.

Along with new styles, new materials were also being developed. In 1907, Leo Baekeland, a Belgian chemist, created a material that, like glass, could be formed and heated with pressure from a mixture of carbonic acid and formaldehyde that solidified into a porous, moldable mass; this new resin was called Bakelite. After 1920, the use of Bakelite found its way into consumer products. When mixed with wood cellulose, the resin could be cast into durable knobs for residential projects. These new materials and designs caught on quickly with designers and hardware manufacturers created colorful handles for cabinets and bath fixtures.

Acrylic resins invented in the 1930s—early trade names were Lucite and Plexiglas—were used in a number of architectural designs. Other materials also gained popularity in the kitchen and bath such as porcelain enamel over rust-resistant surfaces. Although the Art Deco style was embraced in the well-heeled houses of the world—Maison de Verre in Paris and Eltham Palace in London—it did not translate into the mass housing market. Today, there is a revival of the style.

Many hardware manufacturers are reproducing the Art Deco shapes into handles, knobs, and pulls for the streamlined look. Although new materials are being introduced, custom-designed Art Deco homes still feature brass and bronze hardware in bold, graceful shapes. Art Deco is pushing design to yet another level—right into the future.

The Art Deco designs of the 1920s and 1930s were a departure from all past design motifs. This Art Deco–inspired kitchen showcases decorative Deco pulls with the ziggurat or stepped design.

Modern: 1930s to 1950s

The influences and legacies of European Modern movement architects—Richard Neutra, Rudolph Schindler, Ludwig Mies van der Rohe, and Walter Gropius—changed the residential landscape both in Europe and America. Architects wanted to break from the past and find new designs tied to advances in industry and technology. In 1919, Walter Gropius, founder of Germany's Bauhaus School (dedicated to avant-garde design concepts), said, "The Bauhaus believes the machine to be the modern medium of design and [the school] seeks to come to terms with it." He believed that design could be integrated with technology. The first houses to put these philosophies into practice were architect-designed and completely original. Vernacular traditions gave way to functionality and progressive use of materials. Architects designed houses that featured rectilinear forms; modern building methods and materials included poured concrete, curtain walls, cantilevered roofs, and plate glass windows. Simple utilitarian handles and levers in chrome-plated steel graced doors, while wire pulls and plain, round chrome knobs adorned cabinets.

Modern design for the masses did not fully take shape until after World War II when soldiers came home and needed a place to live with their young families. Many of the avant-garde Bauhaus architects such as Gropius had fled Nazi Germany and took positions at the most prestigious architectural schools in the United States; they shaped the lessons of design for a generation of architects. The Modern style could mass-produce standardized building parts, making them affordable for all. Compact box houses with open floor plans and no ornament became standard. The furnishings followed the clean forms of the Modern house.

Designers such as Eero Saarinen, husband and wife team Charles and Henry Eames, and Nelson Miller produced sleek, futuristic designs for the home. The most successful was the Henry Miller furniture

Modern-Inspired

If you have an authentic or Modern-inspired home:

KNOBS AND LEVERS: chrome-plated steel

HINGES: steel butt hinges

CABINET HARDWARE: plastic, steel, geometric shapes, sleek bar pulls

Neutra-style house numbers add a Modern touch to entryways.

Plastic was a popular material in modern spaces. This contemporary kitchen sports small black pulls that contrast against warm wood and cool mesh cabinets.

company that mass-produced these new forms for the growing suburbs. The hardware was as futuristic as the furniture. Clean, geometric shapes molded from aluminum and stainless steel made up the majority of the hardware on such pieces. Simple, elongated bar shapes reflected the utility of the forms. Designers played with boomerang- and saucer-shaped hardware as well.

Mies van der Rohe's less-is-more philosophy was taken to the extreme during this time. Function trumped form in every sense, and in a way, we had come full circle.

Contemporary: 1960s to Present

By the 1970s, a restoration movement in the United States was spurred by such preservationists as Clem Labine who cranked out a monthly newsletter called *Old-House Journal*. Hardware manufacturers saw the turning tide and began to create reproduction designs from a host of past style eras. Early Colonial and Victorian hardware designs popped up in catalogs and hardware stores. By the 1980s, the Arts and Crafts Revival took hold and today every big-box shop and online catalog sells the Craftsman look.

Architects, jewelry designers, and interior designers are also creating masterpieces in hardware, maturing the craft of hardware design into a high art form. Carl Martinez creates beautiful saucer shapes in bronze, while architect James Cutler designs levers and knobs in a mixed media of wood and steel. The traditional design movement has also gained momentum with architects, including noted traditional architect Russell Versaci, who is designing a line of reproduction hardware inspired by nineteenth-century forms.

Today, there is a hardware style to fit every taste and budget—from the futuristic hardware line designed by progressive architects to recasting Victorian forms in to colorful, beaded drawer handles.

Contemporary–Inspired

If you have a Contemporary–inspired home:

KNOBS: stainless steel, aluminum, wood, glass

HINGES: Harmon, butt, olive knuckle

CABINET HARDWARE: geometric shapes, custom designs

Mix and Match

When mixing and matching hardware styles, stay within the same period or similar design periods. For instance, the Arts and Crafts movement has a lot in common with Revival styles, while Art Deco and Modern use similar materials and shapes. But trying to mix a colonial-style look with a modern theme can leave your interiors looking a bit confused.

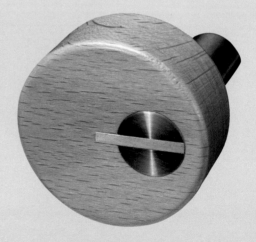

Above: A cutting edge design by James Cutler

Right: Architect James Cutler started creating his own designs when he could not find hardware appropriate for his innovative designs.

Trade Tip

When it comes to antique door hardware there are a few clues to let you know if a piece is the real thing or an imitation:

- Historical roses measure 1¾" (4.5 cm) in diameter and today's roses measure 3" (7.6 cm).

- After 1840, most glass knobs were based in tapered shanks (the cylindrical base of a doorknob that receives the spindle).

- Glass knobs from the turn of the twentieth century were based in stepped threaded shanks.

- In 1870, most shanks were ¼" (0.5 cm) long and spindles were not threaded.

Antique vs. Reproduction

Antique decorative hardware is still plentiful in the marketplace, but many quality pieces have become scarce collectibles and command high prices at auctions. As with most materials, hardware was produced in different grades. In the late 1800s, high-end decorative hardware was either cast in solid brass or bronze—bronze being the more popular material—while lower-end pieces were hollow cast iron with a veneer of bronze or brass. Hollow, cast-iron knobs could cost one-fifth the price of a solid bronze knob. Then, the materials were expensive and the labor was cheap; today, it's just the opposite. Antique hardware can be difficult to work with because it may not be possible to find all the parts you need—for instance, setscrews, spindles, rosettes, and escutcheons for a complete door suite.

Reproduction

They say imitation is the sincerest form of flattery and few industries take this concept to heart more than historical architectural hardware. Several companies produce copies of old designs for today's market, allowing homeowners to purchase matching window latches or several suites of door hardware rather than the one or two they might find through an antiques dealer. Many professional installers prefer to work with reproduction pieces because old hardware doesn't always conform to contemporary building codes or regulations concerning access for the disabled.

The sturdiness of reproduction hardware combined with the classic lines of antique styling is a winning combination.

CHAPTER
Three

Finishing Touches

The type of finish you choose for your architectural hardware offers the final design touch in your home. Much like the way clothing can reflect your mood for the day, a hardware finish can set the tone of your home's decor. Is it bold and high luster or demure and low luster? Along with color preference, there are other considerations to take into account when choosing a finish for your hardware. Should it have a living or organic finish that mellows with age or a lifetime finish that never changes its color from the day you purchased it? In Europe, the preference is to purchase bare metal in iron, bronze, or brass that will mellow and patina with age. In the United States, the tendency is to purchase hardware that has some kind of protective coating, although organic or living finishes are growing in popularity. Whether you have an old house that's hardware is in serious need of an overhaul or you have a new house and want to add a custom finish to stock hardware pieces, a decorative finish can be a cure-all for a multitude of sins.

Elements of Style

When we talk about architectural hardware, the four materials that come up most often are brass, bronze, iron, and stainless steel.

Brass and Bronze

Brass is an alloy of copper and zinc. It has a shiny, yellowish appearance, tarnishes easily when exposed to weather, and is generally protected with a coating of lacquer. The color of the brass may be changed slightly by changing the proportions of the metals and treating the finished castings with acids. Knobs and roses are typically of brass but are often coated with a thin plating of chrome or nickel—two popular choices in the market. Protective coatings include lacquer, a clear powder-coated surface, or a thin layer of chrome or nickel applied using the process of physical vapor deposition (PVD). This process increases surface hardness, scratch resistance, and creates a lifetime guarantee against tarnish. The finish also costs about 50 percent more than a traditional lacquer finish.

The hardware for this doorway is finished in oil-rubbed bronze.

Bronze is commonly an alloy of copper and tin. It is less malleable and harder than brass and is easier to cast. It also oxidizes more easily than brass and so can be offered in a wider array of colors than brass. Many high-end hardware manufacturers let the natural color of bronze make a bold design statement. For instance, silicon bronze contains copper, silicon, and zinc, creating a copper color. White bronze is composed of copper, manganese, nickel, and zinc, producing a silver color. Time, touch, and climate all can enhance and change the patina of the bronze, creating a unique hue. Brass and bronze are superior to iron because they are both easily cast and can yield intricate details when formed from a well-made pattern and mold.

If you want to keep the look of brass or bronze without it oxidizing, modern synthetic coating treatments such as anodizing can be applied. Anodizing forms a protective and uniform oxide on the metal, giving it a hard, tough skin. A variety of color-anodized finishes are available such as black and oxidized bronze.

Iron

Iron is one of the earliest materials used. A pliable metal when subjected to extreme heat, today wrought iron is typically employed for custom and reproduction strap hinges and thumb latches made by blacksmiths. Iron is hard to cast because it melts at such a high temperature, but with a small percentage of aluminum added to the iron, an alloy is formed that melts at a reduced temperature, offering a degree of fluidity in making a casting.

This cast iron alloy melts at a low temperature and offers a casting with sharp detail. Cast iron hardware is always finished because it will rust easily if it is left in its natural state. Zinc has long been used in architectural hardware as a coating over iron and steel because it resists rust. Many products are made using die-cast zinc as a base metal. It is easily cast, machined, and plated.

Stainless Steel

Stainless steel is an iron product and there are about 40 standard types. Each contains substantial amounts of chromium and small quantities of a number of other elements. The majority also contains nickel. Because it is rust resistant, finishes with a high luster, and is easily maintained, stainless steel is a popular choice for architectural hardware.

This lever is finished in polished nickel for a contemporary look.

Trade Tip

PVD is best for hardware on coastal houses where the salt air can speed tarnishing.

Types of Finishes

There are several types of finishes for hardware: polished brass, oil-rubbed bronze, brushed nickel, satin nickel, polished nickel, matte antique brass, burnished antique brass, chrome, zinc—need I go on? There is literally a finish for every type of design style. A natural finish takes on the color of the base metal, for example, brass or bronze. The natural finish can be protected with a lifetime finish. A living finish is a finish that will change through time as oils from your hands and changes in climate react with the finish to create the look of patina and age.

Oil-rubbed bronze, with its dark rich hue, is a great finish for an Arts and Crafts style house, while polished chrome, with its cool, futuristic qualities, is perfect for a sleek, modern townhouse. It's better to stay with one finish when purchasing hardware for your room design, but to add interest, mix the shape of hardware used in the space. Nickel-plated iron was popular 100 years ago for kitchens and baths and is still a good choice for a period-inspired look because it holds up well in these high-moisture areas. The most popular finishes today are the chromiums, both polished and satin.

Mix and Match Finishes

Most designers stay with one type of finish for a room's hardware. Also, a hierarchy of hardware can be introduced, placing the more decorative finishes in the public areas of the home such as the living room and dining room, while having the more modest hardware finishes in the private areas of the house such as the bathrooms and bedrooms.

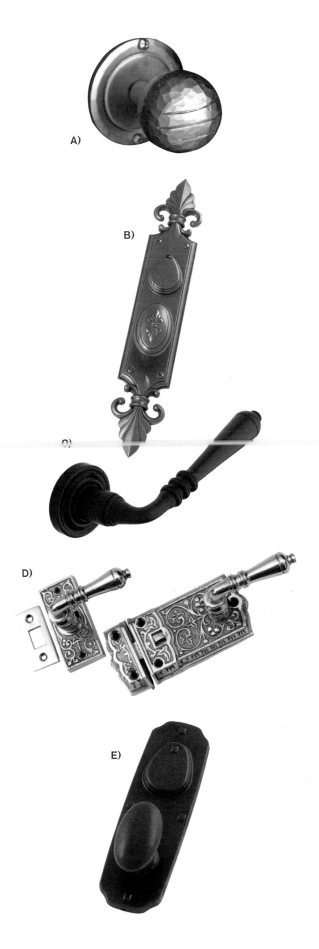

A)

B)

C)

D)

E)

This group of hardware shows an array of finishes: **A)** pewter; **B)** nickel; **C)** oil-rubbed bronze; **D)** polished brass; **E)** white bronze finished with a black patina.

Cleaning Old Hardware

One of the easiest ways to spruce up your existing hardware is to simply clean it. When nonferrous metals such as brass, silver, and copper react with the air's oxygen and sulfur, they tarnish. In this chemical reaction, the surface metal oxidizes turning a dull green—think of the green coating on statues in public parks. If an oxidized surface further reacts with moisture you will get a protective coating or patina—this may or may not be desired.

Hardware is either solid or plated. To determine which type exists on your house, scratch the back of the hardware with a sharp object. If what appears is the same color as on the front, then the piece is solid. If it is plated, a different color will be visible; if you see yellow, it is brass; if you see red, it is bronze. Another way to determine what your hardware is made of is to put a magnet next to the metal. If it sticks, it has an iron base, and if it doesn't stick, you have a nonferrous metal, such as copper or brass.

Before you attempt to polish your brass, test to see if it has a lacquer finish. With a soft cloth, apply polish to an inconspicuous area. The cloth will turn black if the piece is not lacquered. But if there is no color change, the piece is lacquered. Try to save this protective coating by simply dusting with a soft cloth. Don't use water on lacquer because the finish will cloud.

Metal Cleaning 101

Tools and Materials

- Cotton balls
- Cotton swabs
- Needle-nose pliers
- Masking tape
- Soft cloths
- Metal polish
- Protective gloves

1.
To clean a tarnished piece in place, protect the surrounding woodwork by covering it with a low-tack painter's tape. If you remove the hardware, use penetrating oil to loosen the screws. Keep track of which hardware belongs to which door by placing each set in a plastic bag marked with its location.

2.
Test an area to make sure the metal is what you think it is and not lacquered or plated. To clean small items such as screws, hold the screw with the needle-nose pliers while you polish the head.

3.
For highly decorative pieces, use cotton swabs to get in the crevices. Never use a toothbrush when cleaning metal; the plastic bristles can scratch the surface. Steel wool can also become embedded in softer metals and should be reserved for steel. Rinse and dry your hardware and it will sparkle like new.

Many salvage yards sell old dirty hardware that with a little elbow grease can look as good as new again.

Trade Tip

Metals with a patina are not meant to be polished such as on art bronze pieces with a "living finish." Also be careful not to spray products with ammonia, which will attack metal hardware—this is particularly important when washing windows where your sash locks can be ruined. A soft cloth such as a chamois works best for dusting. You can also just polish the raised ornament on a decorative piece to highlight the design. Allow your brass drawer pulls that get a lot of wear to develop a patina—this way you won't be obsessing about keeping them bright and shiny.

Removing Paint

If your hardware has been spattered with paint, don't use a paint stripper to remove it—the chemicals may compromise and even remove the electroplating. An old trick is to shock the metal in hot water, which makes it expand and breaks the bond with the paint. Add two tablespoons of baking soda (a gentle cleansing agent) to a pot of boiling water. Drop in your door handles, rosettes, and hinges. Leave the hardware in the boiling water for a minute or so then take them out and quickly brush off the paint with a low-abrasive scouring pad. If the paint rehardens, place the hardware back in the pot of boiling water. The boiling water bath is safe for most plated and solid metals. To finish off the project, rub a thin coat of beeswax polish on the hardware and reinstall the hardware.

Don't get obsessive about keeping all your hardware shining; cleaning them once a year should suffice. You can apply beeswax compatible with your favorite cleaning product to extend the time between cleanings. If you are unable to keep up with the tarnish, have your pieces lacquered by a reputable plater. Today's spray lacquers found at your hardware store often lack the amount of retarders—due to chlorofluorocarbon regulations—needed to do the job. If not done properly, moisture can get trapped under the lacquer and create a cloudy effect. If you have your hardware professionally finished with a lacquer coating, the hardware should be tarnish free for about ten years.

Don't fret if your new paint job ended up on more than the door. A quick dip in a boiling bath of water can help shock the paint off the hardware leaving it pristine once again.

Replating Hardware

Do you have a house full of dingy, old hardware and think it would be easier to trash it than to restore it? Put down that trash can! There's a solution that could save you money in the long run. Send your historical hardware to a plater. Electroplating metal finishes on hardware has been around since the mid 1800s.

Electroplating is when a cast iron, steel, or other base metal is coated with a finer, more expensive metal to give it the appearance of that metal. Electricity is applied to two metals in a solution. Through a DC current, the thin plate metal is applied to the base metal. When the plating wears thin, the base metal shows through. If your hardware is highly detailed, tarnished, or some of the plating has worn away, send your hardware to a plater. When working with a plater, request to see examples of their finished work. A plater will first strip the hardware of lacquer, paint, or varnish down to its base metal. The most common way platers strip hardware today is by showering the hardware with tiny beads of glass. This leaves less-hazardous waste to dispose of after the piece has been stripped. Once stripped, the piece is polished to remove surface imperfections. After polishing, the base metal is struck with copper to help the plate adhere to the base metal. The hardware is then plated. The plate is polished to achieve its final appearance. The final step for many pieces of hardware is a lacquer coat or a lifetime finish. Your 100-year-old hardware will beam once again.

Trade Tip

If you are restoring a large number of knobs in your home, bag each knob in a separate plastic bag and mark the bag with a name or number. For example, "kitchen side door." This will make it easier to reinstall the pieces after they are returned from the plater.

Trade Tip

When specifying hardware finish colors, refer to the Builder's Hardware Manufacturer's Association (BMHA) standards.

View online at www.buildershardware.com

CHAPTER Four

Open and Shut Case

It is easier than you might think to change or add architectural hardware to your doors, windows, cabinets, or shutters, which will make your home work more smoothly and better reflect your personal style. When doorknobs and locks have worn out their welcome, replacing them is often the best solution—in fact, installing a new cylinder lockset on a passage door can take as little as a half an hour if you have the right materials and tools at hand. The same goes for cabinet, window, and shutter hardware. If you're tired of looking at those small, shiny brass knobs on your kitchen cabinets that scream 1980, replacing them with vintage-inspired antiqued bronze pulls or modern, geometric, chrome-finished knobs will give your kitchen a more personalized look.

What about those 100-year-old cast iron window fasteners on your original two-over-two Victorian windows that are so rusty the locks no longer operate? Today, reproduction cast iron window locks with decorative sweeps topped in porcelain are abundant in the marketplace and are an easy and inexpensive solution to get your windows operating once again.

Adding operable shutters can also dress up the exterior of your home and adorning those shutters with decorative wrought-iron hardware gives your home's façade a polished, welcoming appeal. And the process of hanging the shutters is simple, as long as you have an extra pair of hands to hold the ladder!

These do-it-yourself projects can seem intimidating if you've never cracked open that emergency toolbox. But these simple weekend tasks can make a world of difference to the overall aesthetic of your interiors and exteriors. When purchasing locksets, hinges, and pulls, most manufacturers supply the screws to install your hardware. Make sure you have received all the hardware pieces and coordinating fasteners before you start your project. Also remember to work safely when using your tools, especially power drills, by wearing protective glasses. We'll explore five quick fixes for your home's hardware that will add decorative details to convey your own artistic expression.

Trade Tip

When purchasing the hardware for your project, remember to buy a few extra pieces in case one is lost or breaks in the future.

Simple bridge pulls and knobs finished in antique bronze give this new butler's pantry cabinetry a historical feel.

How to Install a Lockset

If you are installing a mortise lockset on a door, you will need a mortise drill to create a chiseled hole into the door's edge. This takes about 2½ hours to install and is best left to a professional. Today, many interior doors have standard cylindrical and tubular locksets that can be replaced fairly easily. Most doors come predrilled with a standard dimension bore hole of 3" (7.6 cm) diameter. Contemporary rosettes cover the hole. But if you are installing historical hardware on a new door, do not order a door that is predrilled because antique rosettes are much smaller than today's standard sizes.

Trade Tip

Doorknobs on mortise locksets may become loose over time. To tighten the doorknob, loosen the setscrew on the side of the knob's shank, hold the knob on the opposite side of the door, and turn the loose knob clockwise until it fits snugly. Then tighten the screw until it is sitting against the spindle. If the knob is still loose, the spindle treads may be worn and the spindle will need to be replaced.

Tools and Materials

- Cylinder lockset
- Protective eyewear
- Tape measure
- 2⅛" (5.4 cm)-diameter face bore hole saw
- Electric drill
- ½" (1.3 cm) wood chisel
- ⅛" (3 mm) wood drill bit
- ⅞" (2.2 cm) spade bit
- Pencil
- Utility knife
- Screwdriver

Time: 30 minutes

1.
First, remove an existing lockset by unscrewing it from the rosette. If there are no screws visible, look for a small slot in the shank of the knob, push a small screwdriver into that slot, this action will release the knob and trim.

2.
Unscrew and remove the mounting plate as well as the latch faceplate.

3.
Insert the new latch and faceplate into existing the hole.

How to Install a Tubular Lockset on a Predrilled Door

4.
Fasten the faceplate over latch bolt with screws.

5.
Install the inside and outside adapters. Fasten with 1¼" (2.6 cm) flat head screws, but do not tighten them at the same time.

6.
Insert spindle on the diamond. Then slide the bushings onto each spindle and into bore of adapters.

7.
Tighten screws then remove alignment bushings. Remove spindle from latch.

8.
Snap rosettes into place and insert spindle into knob and align setscrew over the marked side of spindle for your door thickness (1⅜" or 1¾" [3.5 or 4.4 cm]).

9.
Insert the spindle and knob into the rosette on the diamond.

10.
While holding the installed knob, push other knob against rosette. Align the hole in handle with the spindle. Insert setscrew and tighten with the Allen wrench.

Fixing a Doorknob

If your lockset is not behaving properly, the lock may be dirty and needs a good cleaning, or it may be dry and needs lubricant. Graphite is the best lubricant to use on door hardware. If the latch bolt does not operate smoothly, the door may not be properly aligned. Watch where the strike plate hits the bolt—is it above, below, or to the side? Scratches from the bolt will appear on the strike plate if it is misaligned. Wood also shrinks and swells with the amount of moisture in the air and the door latch may no longer engage with the strike plate. If the misalignment is less than an 1⁄8" (3 mm), file the edges of the plate to enlarge the opening. If the latch does not reach, remove the existing strike plate and add a new one.

For more than an 1⁄8" (3 mm) misalignment, remove the strike plate and enlarge the mortise above or below. Replace the plate, fill the gap with wood putty, and refinish.

How to Install a Strike Plate

Tools and Materials

- Masking tape
- Chisel
- Drill
- Screws

- Utility knife

Time: 45 minutes

1.
Swing door to closed position. Mark exact center point where latch meets doorframe.

2.
Determine the door's thickness. Use template to mark screw holes and correct center points.

3.
Use masking tape to make 1" hole (2.5 cm) from edge of spade bit. Drill ⅞" (2.2 cm) diameter hole 1" (2.5 cm) deep at the center point.

4.
Align strike plate holes with marks. Score chisel guide into doorframe with utility knife.

5.
Chisel within score marks ¹⁄₁₆" (1.6 mm) deep or until strike plate is flush with wood. Using the strike template, drill ⅛" (3 mm) pilot holes for screws.

6.
Fasten strike plate into position with screws.

How to Install a Lockset on an Undrilled Door

Tools and Materials

- Cylinder lockset
- Protective eyewear
- Tape measure
- 2⅛" (5.14 cm) -diameter face bore hole saw
- Electric drill
- ¾" (1.9 cm) wood chisel
- ⅛" (3 mm) wood drill bit
- ⅞" (2.2 cm) spade bit
- Pencil
- Utility knife
- Screwdriver

Time: 45 minutes

1.

Most locksets come with templates and instructions. Measure 36" to 38" (91.4 to 96.5 cm) from the floor then position the centerline of the template on the height line and mark the center point of the door's thickness and center point for 2⅛" (5.14 cm) hole.

2.

Use a hole saw to bore a 2⅛" (5.14 cm) hole at the point marked on both sides of the door.

3.

As soon as the guide bit exits the opposite side of the door, begin to drill from the other side of the door.

4.

Bore a 1" (2.5 cm) latch hole into edge of door at the center point on the height line using a spade bit at the pencil mark from the template.

5.

Hold a ¾" (1.9 cm) chisel at a 45-degree angle with the beveled edge toward the wood. Working from the center of the mortise, tap the chisel to the bottom and then to the top. The mortise should be ⅛" (3 mm) deep. Insert the faceplate. Remove only a small bit of wood at a time. Follow steps 4 through 6 shown on page 65 to install door hardware.

6.

Insert latch into door and score chisel guides into the door edge using a utility knife. Make sure score lines are parallel to the door. Remove the latch.

Replacing interior doorknobs in your home can make a world of difference to the overall design aesthetic.

How to Replace a Window Sash Fastener

When it comes to older windows, one of the biggest problems is that the fasteners can become loose and worn over time and can allow air leaks and moisture into the home. The locks may be loose and no longer offer security. Although the crescent-cam sash lock is still a popular style for window hardware, manufacturers are offering a number of decorative fasteners and locks to accommodate your window style. And they are as easy as one-two-three to replace.

Replacing a Window Sash Fastener

Tools and Materials

- Screwdriver
- Screws
- Window hardware

- Wood putty

Time: 15 Minutes (plus drying time for putty)

1.
Remove existing hardware with the appropriate screwdriver.

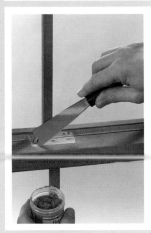

2.
Fill in screw holes with wood putty and let dry.

3.
Fasten the new window hardware with the supplied screws.

4.
The sash lock will keep your window secure for years to come.

Cam sash locks are ubiquitous fixtures on double hung windows. There are several reproduction designs on the market today to fit every house style.

How to Install Cabinet Hardware

One of the easiest and least expensive ways to add sparkle to kitchen cabinets or ho-hum dressers is to replace the hardware. As with many trends these days, anything goes—from Colonial wooden buttons to Victorian bin pulls to contemporary novelty hardware such as metal fish, pineapples, or seashells shapes. But matching sets of hardware—pulls, back plates, and hinges—is the most common approach.

The ideal replacement hardware for your old cabinet fittings will have the same boring dimensions—the distance between the centers of the screw holes. Careful measuring will help determine the appropriate pull or handle size. If you're not able to find the hardware with the same boring dimensions, use a back plate with the new handles to cover the old screw holes. Almost all cabinet knobs, pulls, and handles come with fastening screws, but if you are going for a historically appropriate look in your kitchen, you will want to use slotted screws (This, of course, won't be a problem if you fasten the handles from the inside of the drawer.) The easiest way to mark cabinets and drawers for the placement of hardware is to use a jig mark. This handy tool will save time and give a more accurate measurement. Before beginning a project, double-check how many pulls and knobs you will need. It can be a hassle to get halfway through a project and realize you don't have enough back plates or pulls for the number of cabinets in your kitchen.

Hardware is the finishing touch to cabinets and drawers and should be well integrated with the overall design. The hardware should complement, rather than compete with, the piece. For instance, hammered Craftsman pulls look great against a natural wood tone but are less appropriate for a brightly painted cabinet.

Trade Tip

As a rule, hardware pulls and knobs should be no wider than half of the cabinet door's rail width. Otherwise, the hardware can look overwhelming and out of proportion with the rest of the space.

How to Install Drawer Handles

Tools and Materials

- Hardware: back plate, handle, and screws
- Screwdriver
- Wood putty
- Marking jig
- Masking tape

- Awl
- Drill
- Matching bits
- Wood clamp
- Scrap wood

Time: 10 minutes per drawer

1.
Remove old hardware with screwdriver.

2.
Fill holes with wood putty.

3.
The jig makes it easy to align your hardware properly. Place a piece of wood at the mounting distance of the drawer's top edge. Find the setting on the jig that correlates to the center-to-center mark on the pulls you are installing. Match the marks to the jig on the line. Tighten the knobs to secure the wood to the drawer's top edge.

4.
Mark the drawer with a vertical strip of masking tape at the center of the drawer front. Match the centerline of the jig to the drawer's centerline. Then mark the pull's screw holes with a scratch awl.

5.
Once you have marked the drawer, use a portable drill with the correct bit sized for the screw and drill the first hole into the drawer from the outside. Avoid splintering the inside face of the drawer by clamping a piece of scrap wood inside the drawer.

6.
Use the supplied screws to install the pulls. Be careful not to over tighten the screws.

7.
Once installed, this drawer pull adds a touch of Arts and Crafts aesthetic to the cabinetry.

Shutter Hardware

Adding decorative shutter hardware to your home's exterior can accentuate its curb appeal. The subtle details of a black wrought iron strap hinge or shutter dog can offer charm for your windows. There are many styles of shutters and shutter hardware to choose from, so we'll focus on the most common types of shutter hardware: the strap hinge and the shutter fastener.

Tools and Materials

- Plate pintle and strap hinges
- Pencil
- Level
- Measuring tape
- Screwdriver
- Drill

Time: 30 minutes

1.

Hold the shutter in place in the window casement in its closed position and allow for a ¼" (6 mm) gap between the shutter and the casement at the top, bottom, and side of the shutter. (Placing a ¼" [6 mm] shim under the shutter and another between the casement and sill will allow you to do this more easily).

2.

Assemble the pintle and the strap hinge. Position the pintle on the casement by centering the strap hinge on the shutter's upper rail. Slide the pintle and strap hinge horizontally so the bend in the strap hinge is directly over the inner edge of the casement. Mark the spot.

3.

Remove the shutter and mount the pintle on the mark.

How to Install a Narrow-Plate Pintle and Strap Hinge

4.

With a level, draw a plumb line from the installed pintle down to where the shutter's lower rail will be. Follow step 2 to find the position of the pintle, centering it on the lower rail's shutter. Mark the spot.

5.

Mount the pintle on the spot marked.

6.

Place the shutter back into the window casement, allowing for the ¼" (6 mm) gap described previously.

7.

Place the strap hinges on their respective pintles and swing them around to lay flush and level on the shutter.

8.

Mark the fastener holes on the shutter.

9.

Remove the shutter and mount the strap hinges on the shutter.

10.

Once the strap hinge is fastened, hang the shutter on the pintles. *Voila*, you have new shutters.

Installing a Shutter Fastener

Shutter fasteners, pivoted devices used to hold a shutter in the open position on the exterior side of the window, add beauty and practicality for operating shutters. They should be placed near the outer, lower corner of the shutter. A good reference point is to have the head contact the shutter 4" (10.2 cm) in from the outer edge and 1" (2.5 cm) up from the bottom edge of the shutter. Fasteners mounted to windowsills are installed after the shutters are hung.

A shutter fastener relies on gravity to work. The larger, heavier portion of the head is designed to hang straight down, while the smaller portion at the top secures the shutter in an open position.

Shutters and their hardware add the perfect complement to this stone house.

Tools and Materials

- Measuring tape
- Screws
- Drill
- Screwdriver

- Shutter tieback

Time: 30 minutes

1.
To position a sill-mounted fastener, open your shutter and place the fastener so that the upper, retaining part of the head will overlap and hold the shutter open.

2.
Once you select the position, be sure the sill-mount bar is level and mark its holes onto the windowsill.

3.
Attach the sill-mount assembly using the appropriate wood screws. Make sure that the fastener's head can swing freely and rests in a position that will hold the shutter securely.

PART TWO
Design Details

How many of us have simply stuck with what our general contractor or home-builder specified for the architectural hardware in our homes because we just didn't know we had a choice? Architectural hardware is not only functional but can add style and personality to our living spaces. Often referred to as the jewelry of architectural elements, hardware choices are limitless. Whether you're going for a period approach or an ultramodern palette, you will surely find the right style of hardware for your project. In this section, we'll explore how designers add architectural hardware to a variety of rooms—from the living room to the home office and from the kitchen to the bath—allowing function and form into our homes.

CHAPTER Five

Kitchen Accoutrements

The workhorses of the kitchen, architectural hardware will get more wear and tear in this room than any other room in the house. This said, function must play a key role in the design decision. Whether you are matching a historical style or creating a contemporary look, the hardware must be sturdy enough to withstand the amount of use it will receive. The earliest colonial American cabinet fasteners were simple, wood-turned buttons. Pressed metal became available with the advent of the Industrial Revolution. Brass bin pulls, cupboard catches, and cabinet knobs appeared in butler's pantries and kitchens in the mid-1800s. Nickel plating became popular in late nineteenth-century kitchens because it didn't tarnish in these typically moist rooms. Today's resurgence of Victorian-era pieces finds reproductions at the big-box home centers and specialty hardware suppliers.

Architects Charles and Henry Greene, who were instrumental in defining the American Arts and Crafts aesthetic, designed the famous 1909 Gamble House in Pasadena, California, an ideal example of kitchen cabinetry designed with elongated, wood drawer pulls. Modest homes of the 1920s featured colored or clear glass kitchen cabinet knobs, which several contemporary companies are also reproducing.

The modern, sleek look of chrome-plated kitchen cabinet handles and hinges emerged in the 1930s. At the same time, Bakelite, a popular plastics manufacturer, produced brightly colored knobs and pulls that gave the kitchen a playful look. Along with the metal kitchen cabinets introduced in the 1940s came simple aluminum hardware in strong geometric shapes. As Tudor and Colonial Revival styles flourished during the 1930s and 1940s, so too did creative ideas for kitchen cabinet hardware. Reproduction hammered pieces and strap hinges continued well into the kitsch 1950s and '60s. Today, mid-twentieth-century modern is making a comeback and many of the original companies continue to manufacture these utilitarian designs. Whatever your kitchen style, the hardware you choose should not only accent that style but be functional and sturdy.

Trade Tip

Door and drawer pulls in a kitchen should be operable with one hand, require only a minimal amount of strength for operation, and not require tight grasping, twisting, or pinching of the wrist.

Architect John B. Murray designed this high-rise kitchen. Using a standard cabinet design of the 1910s, Murray incorporated nickel olive knuckle hinges into the door design for a highly stylized effect. He continues the nickel finish on the simple cabinet knobs.

Vintage-Inspired Farmhouse

The kitchen and butler's pantry looks like an antiquated space in this Greek Revival farmhouse. Although it appears to be very old, it is part of a five-year-old home designed by architect Gil Schafer III. A perfectionist in every way, Schafer designed this farmhouse kitchen with historically appropriate details—right down to the kitchen cabinet hardware. Using simple, straightforward forms based on late nineteenth-century butler's pantries, the cabinets have flat, glass-front panels. Schafer chose to use the cupboard catches and bin pulls that were ubiquitous 100 years ago. Instead of purchasing top-of-the-line pulls for these service areas, he purchased simple, inexpensive cupped pulls in brass and had them replated in antique brass. This approach gave Schafer the custom look he wanted without the high cost. Schafer also used the same finish for the cupboard cabinet catches, window hardware, cabinet hinges, and towel rack, thereby creating a unified look. The hardware complements the simplicity of the design. The period finish offers another layer of historically accurate detailing to the room. Also used in the house are flush-mounted window lifts—popular in older homes—lending the impression that this is a house that has stood on the land for centuries.

Design Details

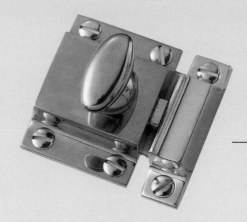

The original shiny brass finish was given an antique brass look.

The flush-mounted window lifts, a component on late 1800s windows, add authenticity to the room.

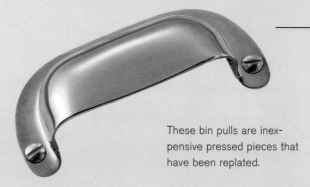

These bin pulls are inexpensive pressed pieces that have been replated.

Architect Gil Schafer incorporated bin pulls and cupboard catches in the design of his new Greek Revival farmhouse kitchen. The hardware is plated in antique brass, giving the impression of age.

Seeing Red

When homeowners David Lans and Lynne Doll bought this 1928 Spanish Colonial home, its kitchen was in serious need of renovation. The 1960s brown cabinet doors were falling off their faux strap hinges and the appliances were outdated. Lans and Doll had complete respect for the age of this Mediterranean-style house and wanted to reinvent its past. They decided to re-create a kitchen that would honor the house's age. Lans hired designer Liza Kerrigan to help him with his vision. While Kerrigan hit the drawing board to design the kitchen, Lans went in search of cabinet hardware. He found dozens of vintage Bakelite knobs and handles from the era and purchased the lot. The simple, red, curved hardware handles play off a repetitive red dot found in the backsplash border. Punches of red became the color accent in the kitchen. The china cupboard's leaded glass-front cabinets received a sprinkling of diamond-shaped panes of glass. So as not to compete with this strong colorful detail, Kerrigan installed simple glass knobs—ubiquitous in 1920s kitchens—on the china cupboard. Adding a mix of materials and color to the space makes an eye-catching statement.

Kerrigan advises using the proper hinges when hanging cabinet doors. She has seen clients make the mistake of incorporating metal cabinet hinges that have no adjustment tolerances for wood. When the hinges were put onto wood cabinets that swelled, contracted, and settled, the hardware had to be continually adjusted.

Design Details

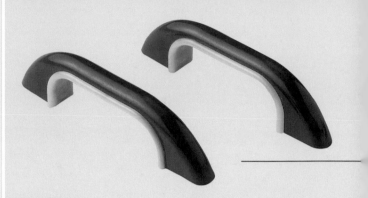

The vintage red, curved, Bakelite pulls trimmed in cream add the appropriate 1920s feel.

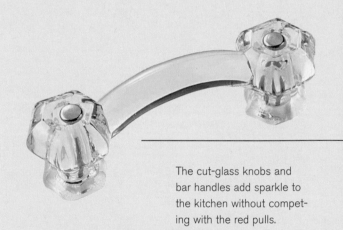

The cut-glass knobs and bar handles add sparkle to the kitchen without competing with the red pulls.

Homeowner David Lans found a complete set of old plastic cabinet pulls for his bungalow kitchen cabinets. Glass knobs and bridge pulls complete the 1920s look of the kitchen's china cupboard.

Spanish Eclectic

Old World charm meets contemporary living in this Spanish Colonial kitchen. Homeowner Merle Mardigan wanted to re-create kitchens she had seen on her travels to Europe. To achieve this theme, designer Liza Kerrigan opted out of using above-counter cabinets. To provide enough storage, Kerrigan instead added base cabinets and designed them a little taller than stock cabinetry—38" (96.5 cm) rather than the standard 36" (91.4 cm), and deeper—30" (76.2 cm) rather than the standard 24" (61 cm). This storage unit is a succession of drawers of different sizes, so the hard-working hardware had to be sturdy. Kerrigan chose a simple, utilitarian 3" (7.6 cm) wire pull for its durability. The simple yet sleek drawer pulls and breadboard knobs finished in chrome contrast with the dark cherry wood. For antiquity, Kerrigan added a pair of old, ornately carved Indonesian doors with wrought iron handles to a wall cupboard. New hinges finished in light rust offer patina. Kerrigan also lined the barrel-vaulted passageway to the dining room with concealed pantries that are accessed with touch-latch doors. The outcome is a space where old and new come together in harmony.

Design Details

These iron hinges with a decorative finial in light rust create an Old World look.

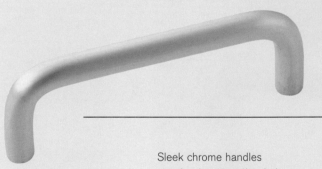

Sleek chrome handles stand out against the dark cherry wood and offer a contemporary feel.

Inspired by European-style kitchens of centuries past, designer Liza Kerrigan incorporated antique Indonesian doors to a storage space. The wrought iron door pulls and hinges finished in light rust evoke the patina of age. In contrast, modern chrome drawer pulls complete the cabinetry.

Arts and Crafts Artistry

Influences of early twentieth-century architectural duo Charles and Henry Greene (who referenced Japanese and Swiss architecture for their own designs) are evident in this new Arts and Crafts kitchen designed by architect Curtis Gelotte. The American Arts and Crafts movement has resurfaced in the current residential design industry and many companies are re-creating the look for homes today. Interior designer Hilary Young chose these simple cabinet fittings reflective of the space's predominantly Asian design. The simple, straightforward lines of the cabinetry are complemented with hammered bridge pulls finished in antique copper. A back plate was added to the upper cabinets' and drawers' hardware to give the design more weight and texture against the warm tones of the vertical grain of the Douglas fir. For a unified design, the antique copper finish carries through to the kitchen windows' sash lifts and into the breakfast nook cubby hardware.

Design Details

Linear forms found in these bridge pulls reflect the American Arts and Crafts movement of the last century.

The rough surface of the back plate suggests they were hand hammered, an effect that completes the Arts and Crafts kitchen.

Designer Hilary Young followed architect Curtis Gelotte's theme when specifying hardware for the kitchen. The hammered back plates add a handcrafted touch to the space, while the antique copper finish adds antiquity.

In the Black

Before kitchen designer Dalia Tamari starts the design process, she asks her clients to fill out a ten-page questionnaire that includes such questions as, "How often do you go grocery shopping?" and "How many cookbooks do you own?" It is questions like these that determine if someone is a passionate cook or how much storage space they will need in the kitchen. For this classic kitchen design in her own penthouse apartment, Tamari worked with Mickey Green to create her dream kitchen. The original kitchen was tiny, so Green turned a bedroom into the kitchen. Green also opened the kitchen to the dining and living rooms. To give the illusion of a larger space, the color scheme was carried through to those additional rooms. The kitchen features partially honed black granite countertops, oak floors painted black, a black La Cornue stove, and black oversized cabinet pulls and knobs. The bail pulls are brushed nickel with a porcelain bead centered on the handle. The shape of the oval pull on the cabinet doors matches the drawer handle. Because of the width of the drawers, each drawer receives two pulls. The hardware adds a bold yet sophisticated statement to the highly polished cooking space. Green advises when purchasing hardware to make sure the hardware is easy to pull —its best to try it out before you purchase. Also make sure that the hardware is easy to clean and does not smudge easily, and, finally, select hardware that is in style with your cabinets.

Design Details

Because of the size of the drawers, Green specified two pulls for each drawer longer than 18" (45.7 cm).

The egg-shaped cabinet doorknobs add a sophisticated touch to the cabinetry.

The black accents in this high-style kitchen are followed through to the smallest hardware details.

Urban Setting

Interior designer Frank Roop creates an original environment each time he designs a living space. To keep his projects fresh, he uses antiques, his own personal designs, or unusual pieces he happens upon. He understands it is important that a home should reflect his client's personality. When designing his own kitchen in a city brownstone, Roop introduced his own personality to the space. Natural and manmade materials are combined to create the ultimate in sophistication, simplicity, and comfort. Carrara marble counters, stainless steel, and birch wood come together in this urban setting. "I wanted to incorporate a seating area in the kitchen, even though the space is small," says Roop. The ceiling height soars and Roop plays with this height through the exaggerated stainless steel ventilation duct. Roop also plays with scale and proportion in the space through the use of oversized clear glass cabinet pulls. The glass doors of the upper cabinetry have simple, modern chrome knobs while the drawers below are outfitted with chunky glass pulls. "I like details that are clean and simple; I don't like overly detailed kitchens," he says. "I think hardware looks best when it is architectural and not embellished." Roop's clever use of natural materials in the space works together in harmony, creating a functional, trend-setting interior.

Design Details

Small button pulls are installed on the glass-front cabinetry.

Chunky glass drawer handles create a striking contrast on wood.

Although the space is small, designer Frank Roop packs the kitchen with textures such as glass and marble.

Euro-Style Meets Country Classic

With the sea just steps away from this beachfront home, designer Mick De Guilio wanted the kitchen to be fresh, clean, and speak to both his clients' tastes. The design evolved by incorporating sleek contemporary cabinetry with country-classic reproduction antiques such as the walnut farmhouse table and country French chairs with rush seats.

Because of the large size of the kitchen, a simple morning station was designed. This is an 8' (2.4 m) station with an icemaker, sink, dishwasher, and wall cabinet storage. It is located close to the table area so that dishes and meals can be efficiently moved from point to point. The coffeemaker and toaster oven are housed in wall recesses, keeping these small appliances clean and out of sight.

Stainless ribbed-front tambour doors were used in the wall cabinetry beneath a composition of stacked four-over-four cabinet doors in a 2' x 2'-square (0.6 x 0.6 sq m) dimension. Rhythmic proportions were used throughout.

An important aspect of the design was to keep all finishes light and make sure that the available natural light enhanced the space. The main work island is a beautiful piece of white stone and the backsplash area also uses the same material.

The cabinetry is of frameless construction with flush-mounted doors. The framework and hinges are concealed inside the cabinetry, giving the island and all cabinets a sleek look. The elongated aluminum drawer pulls are all about function and form.

Design Details

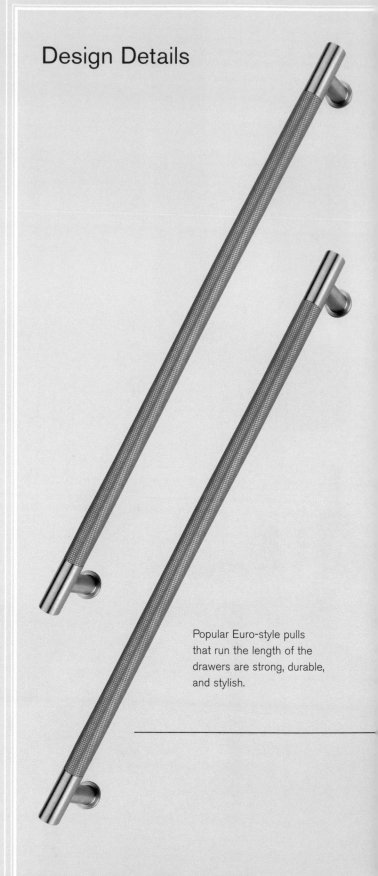

Popular Euro-style pulls that run the length of the drawers are strong, durable, and stylish.

The clean white cabinetry and aluminum pulls are making their way into the American market.

C H A P T E R
Six

Bathroom Basics

Bathrooms are all about luxury. In new homes, bathrooms are getting bigger and better, with more bells and whistles—including hardware. Combined with dressing areas and walk-in closets, some bathrooms have more square footage than even the master bedroom. With the additional square footage being filled with oversized whirlpool bathtubs, steam showers, and radiant floors, the bathroom is beginning to resemble a modern-day Roman spa.

But what type of hardware is appropriate for the bath? Because most homebuilders specify chrome or nickel finishes for faucets, these finishes are the most popular, although style and finish choices are endless. And with today's finish technologies, any look can be achieved in the bathroom. There's a strong trend toward bath hardware finishes going warmer with Venetian bronze. Distressed and antique looks are also gaining popularity. And these warmer finishes have a lacquer coating that can hold up in humid spaces.

Trade Tip

When selecting hardware for the bathroom, choose pieces that will stand up to the high moisture content created by running water, such as those made of nickel, porcelain, painted wood, and glass.

Designers often match the bath hardware finish with the plumbing finish—not just the towel rack but also the trash can and tissue box. To give your bath more personality, think of mixing and matching complementary styles for towel bars, bath baskets, towel warmers, safety or grab bars, doorknobs or levers, and window catches, while keeping the finish consistent throughout the room.

Lever handles are gaining popularity in the household—particularly in the bath where a lever can be easier to open with wet or lotion-coated hands. Many bath showrooms and home centers group bath hardware and accessories together, so you can't go wrong when choosing from the manufacturer's design palette.

This modern bathroom is outfitted with square knobs finished in brushed chrome.

Beach House Bath

After years of neglect, the absentee owner of this beach house was ready to hire the wrecking ball to tear it down and build a brand new home in its place. But while driving around with a real estate agent, Tom Healy and Fred Hochberg took one glimpse and said, "Stop the car. This is the one." Healy closed the real estate deal and went straight to work resurrecting the bedraggled beach house to its former glory—and then some. For the master bath, Healy kept some of the 1950s spirit such as the glass block wall but updated the space with ultramodern fixtures and fittings. The contemporary master bath has two walls of custom cabinetry. Healy custom-designed the cabinets with simple cut outs to act as the hardware—just pull the drawer at the recess and it opens easily. For added security, the original steel casement windows have new utilitarian-style fasteners. The bath is both contemporary and functional.

Design Details

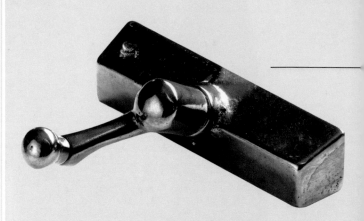

The original casement windows have new casement fasteners for added security.

The bathroom details are luxurious and the design allows for plenty of storage.

Vanity Fair

For this handsome master bathroom in a new home, the designer used a clean, creamy palette contrasted with bold accents. The natural, warm wood tones of the bath surround, floor, and countertops play against the cool stone of the shower stall and its glass door. For a dash of color, the designer chose simple cut-glass, vibrant red knobs installed on the drawers of the double sink vanity. Although around since the early 1800s, this type of glass knob became mainstream in the 1920s and 1930s and was a popular choice for both cabinetry and doorknobs. The playful accents contrast with the sleek chrome-plated hardware—introduced in the early twentieth century—found on the electrical cover plates and towel bar. A modern luxury and a must-have in homes in cooler climates, the towel warmer is also finished in chrome. The designer was not afraid to mix it up in this bath, reminding us to take risks in designing our own bathrooms. A simple change of a knob on your cabinetry can add a bit of color and texture to the room.

Design Details

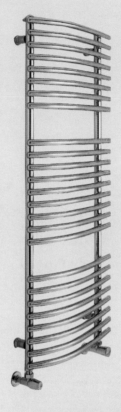

Heated towels warmers are popular in cold-climate bathrooms. The contemporary linear design adds beauty to the bath while keeping towels toasty warm.

The red glass knobs add a bit of color to this bathroom awash with neutral tones.

The designer creates interest in the design of this master bath by mixing materials, colors, and textures.

Cool Finishes

Turn-of-the-nineteenth-century baths inspired this new bathroom, with its cool Carrara marble countertops, tub surround, floors, and sink flanked by two five-drawer built-in cabinets. The homeowner, not wanting to eliminate windows in the design of the space—which would allow natural light to filter into the space—set two small casement windows at ceiling height. The placement of the windows allows for added privacy, ventilation, and wall space for the oversized mirrored medicine cabinet. The cabinetry features simple, polished chrome-plated knobs that complement the gray vein in the marble and match the legs and faucets of the washbasin. The two-tiered towel bar is also finished in a nickel plate to match the cabinet hardware. The designer achieved tranquility and a serene setting for this pretty yet functional bathroom.

Design Details

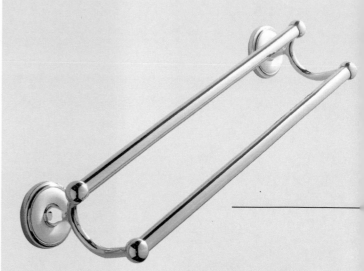

The chrome towel bar is a cool complement to the white marble.

Simple round knobs dress the vanity.

The traditional bath is outfitted with chrome fixtures, a popular choice for the bath today.

1800s Update

Adding bathrooms into homes built before the invention of this necessary element can be challenging to say the least. Often another room in the house has to be sacrificed to create a bathroom. In the restoration of this eighteenth-century farmhouse, the homeowner took a room originally used as a bedroom and created a sensitive bath design in keeping with the house's antiquity. The room's twelve-over-twelve windows were still in tact but needed restoration to get them in working order. The designer chose simple cam sash-lock window fasteners, replacing the rusted iron fittings. She chose a built-in wall unit for added storage—something lacking in homes that predate the closet! The built-in cabinetry's drawers have flat-paneled fronts while the cabinets are finished in bead board. Simple, round, wood knobs are found on chests and cabinets. To give the cabinetry its clean country feel, the designer painted the knobs a pale yellow, the same color as the cabinetry. To the right of the cabinetry is a paneled closet with double doors—another built-in addition to the room. Paying homage to the home's beginnings, the hardware is eighteenth-century reproduction wrought-iron thumb latches and pulls. Instead of a strap hinge, which would have overwhelmed the small closet door, the designer chose simple butt hinges. Note the wooden turn catch on the door—another touch that respects the home's age. The bathroom achieves its modern purpose while not compromising the home's historical integrity.

Design Details

As a reminder of the home's age, the designer introduced reproduction hand-wrought hardware onto the simple paneled door.

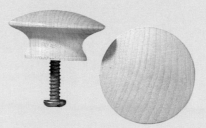

Simple wooden knobs are painted butter yellow to match the cabinetry, which is appropriate for the classic country look.

When working with older homes, choose hardware that is appropriate to the age of the overall home. For instance, decorative Victorian pieces wouldn't look appropriate in a seventeenth-century Shaker-style home.

Boathouse Basics

One of the most sought-after themes in contemporary baths is tranquility: clean lines, soft colors, and a welcoming atmosphere. For this new construction project, architect Eric Reinholdt of Elliott Elliott Norelius, characterizes the house as a modernist interpretation of vernacular coastal architecture.

"This bath was conceived of as a boat interior. Each item was to fit perfectly into a specific location, yet each was to remain expressive of its function, construction, and materiality," explains Reinholdt. The cabinetry was meant to be geometrically clean; when drawers and doors were closed, the lines of the cabinet were to remain pure. This meant that the hardware also had to fit that requirement. The granite surfaces were expressed as thin veneers, wrapping corners and lining shelves and, on the counter, as pure slabs carved away to reveal the lavatories. "The bathroom, as a very private, inwardly focused space, is lit from high clerestories that framed a view into the forest canopy," says Reinholdt. "The materials are warm and dark, and were meant to ground the room as a sheltered space." The lever door handle was critical to the design. "It's expressive of the function of opening a latch and the geometry of extrusion relates directly to the other fixtures chosen for the house, all of which are geometrically simple and understated," continues Reinholdt. The vanity was custom designed by Reinholdt. Its hardware is cast-brass, flush ring pulls in polished chrome; its drawer's ball-bearing drawer slides extend fully. In this particular case, selecting hardware for a small bathroom dictates a little creativity. "I relied on the local boat building tradition for inspiration," he says. "There are many, many options for boat hardware on the market and it's quite often a perfect fit for bathrooms. They conserve space and reference a tradition rooted in beauty and fine craft." Often, bathrooms can be cluttered places, but Reinholdt's preference is to ground those spaces with simple, object like fixtures, hardware, and fittings.

Design Details

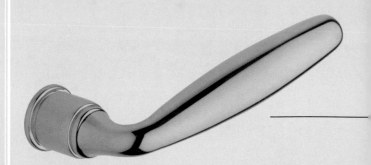

An ADA-compliant lever handle placed 36" (91.4 cm) above the door offers a handsome entry and fits into the geometric design scheme found throughout the house.

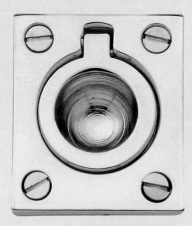

The front of the cabinetry is perfectly flush with its flat-front panels and flush ring pulls. The design offers a clean effect to the space.

Eric Reinholdt's design is based on boat-building techniques. The design is compact and no space is wasted. This philosophy is reflected right down to the flush ring pulls on the vanity.

Country Classic

Everything about this bathroom says relaxed country style—from its painted wood floor in a black-and-white checkerboard pattern to its simple fittings. For this old house bathroom, the homeowner pulled from the past for inspiration to create the country-classic retreat. In keeping with the house's antiquity, the homeowner incorporated simple porcelain knobs used during the 1800s in modest farmhouses or in service or servants quarters. The homeowner matched the antiqued brass finish of the knobs on the vanity cupboard with the finish on the faucet fixtures—a popular treatment when choosing an overall finish for the bathroom. Instead of incorporating a traditional wall-mounted towel rack into the bath space, the homeowner chose simple schoolhouse hooks for hanging towels and washcloths. The light switch plates also match the antiqued brass finish of the cabinets. When creating a country look in the bath, keep your hardware simple and unadorned. Antique finishes work best to create a country cottage feel. Wall-mounted towel bars were not introduced to the bath until the early twentieth century, so the homeowner's choice of hooks is appropriate. Select finishes that will stand up to the moisture in the bathroom. It is best to get reproductions rather than antique pieces for the bath because the reproduction pieces will often have protective coatings, such as a lacquer finish, to protect against moisture, while an antique piece may not.

Design Details

The porcelain knobs were ubiquitous fittings in farmhouses. The white porcelain knob is fitted into a porcelain brass rose.

The coat hooks are employed as towel hooks.

The vanity's brass knobs are in finished antiqued brass.

A country cottage bath design was in order for this antique farmhouse—complete with nineteenth-century porcelain knobs and schoolhouse hooks.

Vintage Victorian

When Rita Shepard purchased the last piece of build-able land in a historic coastal neighborhood, she wanted to make sure every inch of her new home would fit in with the well-established surroundings—right down to the smallest details—even the hardware. Simple antique farmhouses in the area inspired the house. Architect Sandra Vitzthum sited the house on the pie-shaped lot so all the rooms would have views of the water—including the master bath. To outfit the bath with plenty of storage, Vitzthum designed a handsome bird's-eye maple dresser with a marble counter and porcelain sink inspired by late 1900s Victorian dressers. A carpenter built the cabinetry to Vitzthum's specifications. The finishing touch was the cabinet hardware chosen for the historically inspired piece. Vitzthum researched Victorian furniture to determine the most appropriate handles and knobs for the custom cabi-netry. The dresser is outfitted in reproduction nine-teenth-century cast-brass pulls and antiqued brass knobs. The cabinet doors swing on ball-tip cabinet hinges, which are also brass. To play off of the sink and tub faucets, Vitzthum chose the same antique brass finish for the cabinet hardware. Vitzthum's bath design—right down to the cabinet hardware—appears to be from a distant era, perfectly playing out Shepard's plan to have even the smallest details reflect the historical setting where she chose to build her new old house.

Design Details

Each cabinet receives two ball-tip hinges.

The Rosette drawer pull has cast-brass bails and simple, round back plates.

The 1" (2.5 cm) simple, classic knob is also finished in antique brass.

Sandra Vitzthum had this dresser custom-made for her client's master bath.

Old World in the Alps

Les Silènes was built by the Megève architect Aldo Merlin at the foot of the Mont Blanc massif in the Savoy Alps. This French chalet is a tribute to historical chalets in the region. The bright, comfortable wooden house with views of Mont Charvin, the Aiguilles de Varan, and the Aravis mountain ranges is the perfect mountain getaway. All the rooms, including the bathroom of the farmhouse, are rustic in feel. The bathroom is integrated into the rest of the structure with reclaimed hundred-year-old wooden planks. The vanity's hardware is a series of rustic, wrought iron knobs. The doors leading into the narrow bathroom have decorative reproduction wrought iron thumb latches. The Old World look of the door hardware works perfectly with the recycled timber used for the doors, vanity, plank walls, and ceilings. One telltale sign of modernity in the space is the accordion mirror. The architect has achieved a wonderfully rustic interior space—quite fitting for this mountain setting.

Design Details

Wrought iron thumb latches add antique authenticity to the space.

Simple wrought iron knobs dress up the rustic vanity.

This new design, inspired by antique mountain chalets, is outfitted with decorative wrought iron fixtures.

Living Spaces

"If I were asked to say what is at once the most important production of art, and the thing most to be longed for, I should answer, a beautiful house." When William Morris, father of the English Arts and Crafts movement, spoke these words, he undoubtedly meant every aspect of the home, including the home's architectural hardware. Hardware in your living spaces can add another design layer of texture, color, and personality, not to mention function. In fact, it is in these spaces where art and function meet and your interiors can truly sparkle. Whether it's a home office with handsome barrister shelves adorned with delicate brass knobs and a 1930s writer's desk with handsome bail pulls, a great room with an elaborate, custom-designed, built-in home entertainment center with craftsman style handles; or a bedroom dressed in decorative silver Louis XV oval doorknobs, there are a host of designs available to satisfy even the most whimsical tastes.

Many contemporary architects and designers are crossing over into the realm of architectural hardware design including metalsmith Ted Meuhling. He has designed a series of butterfly-shaped drawer pulls. When unevenly spaced on cabinetry, it gives the impression that the butterflies are in motion. Function and artistry come together beautifully.

One of the first steps to determining which type of hardware fits your home's style is to look at the architecture. You wouldn't want to outfit your interior doors with seventeenth-century wrought iron thumb latches if your home is a high-style Victorian. Also, look at the hierarchy of your home's spaces; if you have a formal living room and entertain often, you'll want to reserve the best quality hardware for this space. The same goes for a formal dining room. And remember, the hardware should enhance the design, not compete or disrupt the look you are trying to achieve. When outfitting, say, your child's playroom, you'll want the hardware to be durable enough to take the wear and tear of the space, but you don't have to purchase top-of-the-line fixtures with custom finishes. It's safe to say most kids won't know the difference!

Whether you're involved in a new construction project or remodeling your home, leave a line item for each room's hardware. The specifications should include the style, color, finish, and patina. These specifications should be finalized before the doors, windows, and cabinetry are ordered. Working with an architect or an interior designer can help you narrow down your hardware choices. But remember, function and form must go hand in hand!

Whether your living room is relaxed or formal, there is a hardware style to fit your personal taste.

Medieval Inspiration

When Sandra Vitzthum designed this new old house inspired by English Arts and Crafts design, she incorporated medieval touches throughout the space. The homeowner, Charlie Hayes, a collector of Arts and Crafts antiques, wanted a home that would show off the Arts and Crafts handcraft materials used in the home. For this simple guest bedroom, Vitzthum designed a closet of simple bead board. Its door has functional 18"(45.7 cm) wrought-iron strap hinges and a bean-shaped thumb latch. The black wrought-iron strap hinges play off the leaded glass casement windows in the room. "In order to be functional, the strap hinge needed to be that length to carry the weight of the door," says Vitzthum. The restrained design of the hardware fits well into the tranquil space, which includes reproduction William Morris paper, an antique spindle bed with white cotton bedspread, and simple white curtains. The handcrafted hardware is a perfect tribute to the Arts and Crafts movement prevalent throughout the space—William Morris would definitely approve.

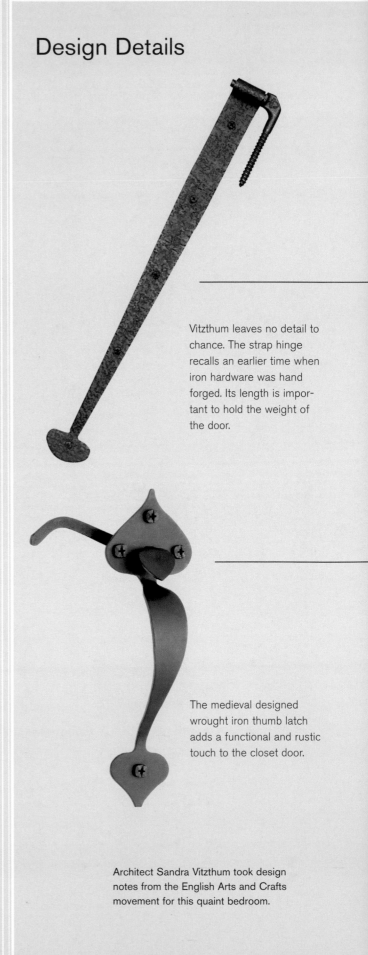

Vitzthum leaves no detail to chance. The strap hinge recalls an earlier time when iron hardware was hand forged. Its length is important to hold the weight of the door.

The medieval designed wrought iron thumb latch adds a functional and rustic touch to the closet door.

Architect Sandra Vitzthum took design notes from the English Arts and Crafts movement for this quaint bedroom.

Log Cabin Fittings

A natural fit in northern pine forests, this log cabin is the perfect rustic getaway for an active, outdoorsy couple who love to entertain. The log home has the feeling of a rustic mountain chalet—with its the hand-peeled red and yellow pine timbers acting as member supports. The kitchen opens out to a dining area with a series of casement windows and doors. The buffet counter is topped in local granite and has box-frame cabinetry with twig cabinet pulls. The pulls are yellow pine with a protective varnish. To further the rustic look of the space, no two pulls are alike. The clever handles play off the natural shape of the kitchen table and chair legs. The knot-filled irregularity of the timbers used in the home shows the care applied to the smallest details.

Design Details

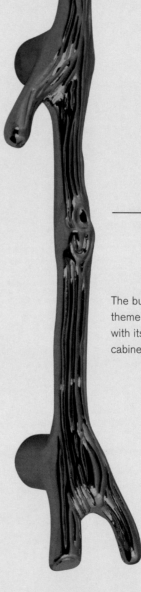

The buffet picks up the theme of the house design with its twig drawer and cabinet pulls.

Every detail in this log cabin home says the great outdoors—even the cabinet pulls.

Farmhouse Guesthouse

It's hard to imagine that this charming little guest cottage's sitting room was once a tannery. Built in the 1820s as part of a farmstead, the old stone building was converted to guest quarters by architect Greg Wiedemann. His challenge was to update the space to make it cozy for visiting friends and family while still maintaining the integrity of the antique building. The stone structure had much of its charm still intact—quarried limestone, clapboard siding, and English ivy climbing its walls. Wiedemann focused most of his efforts on the interiors. With preservation always in mind, he devised ways to update the interior for twenty-first century living without compromising the interior's integrity. He designed built-in cupboards and cabinets to hide wiring throughout the house—likening the experience to threading a needle. He also chose historically appropriate hardware for doors and cabinetry throughout the tiny space. Wiedemann drew inspiration for the hardware from the early nineteenth-century wrought iron H-shaped hinges found on an original closet. He chose to replicate the H-shaped hinges for other doors and cabinets in the space as well as to introduce Suffolk thumb latches for the doors, which are appropriate to the building's age. In caring about the smallest details in the structure, Wiedemann was able keep the buildings character intact. One can imagine that a local blacksmith hand-hammered the hardware pieces at the local forge—a tribute to the architect's craft at play in this simple country guesthouse.

Design Details

The L-hinge offers added support to the antique doors and can be found on all doors of this simple stone guesthouse.

An H-shaped hinge supports the middle of the door.

The Suffolk thumb latch is also a centuries old design that complements the iron hinges.

Where original architectural elements were missing in this 200-plus-year-old structure, architect Greg Wiedemann had them reproduced.

European Sophistication

Zurich-based interior designer Susanne von Meiss has learned her business from experience. She has traveled the world and seen hundreds of houses and interiors through the critical eye of a journalist. Her own home is an expression of her extensive world travels. Cool, natural tones and materials mixed with an eclectic array of antiques—ranging from Gustavian to Biedermeier—fill the space.

In one corner of the drawing room stands a desk in linen stone and a silk-covered stool. The simple, bronze desk-drawer handle breaks the line of the desk front, adding visual interest to the piece. The oversized, paned casement windows and doors in the room are outfitted with elegant scroll-handle casement fasteners in cast iron. The fasteners are the perfect complement to the elegant windows and the Fortuny silk taffeta drapery flanking them. The round mirror is a mid-twentieth-century piece from the Grand Hotel Dolder in Zurich. The Burmese monks are a find from Thailand. The hardware is understated and functional. It does not jump out of the space but simply adds a quiet decorative touch to the overall design.

Design Details

The casement windows fasten with a decorative scroll handle. These reproduction pieces offer another layer of antiquity to the space.

The simple drawer pull on the desk is in the same finish as the window fasteners.

The room is elegant, and its elements are an eclectic mix of finds from around the world. The designer ties the architectural hardware together in the room through color and texture.

Child's Play

If there is one space in your home that you can have fun designing, it's your children's rooms. It's where your imagination can soar and where you can help your child's imagination soar, too! One key point to remember is that the nursery is a place of growth, so you don't want to create a design in the space that is only appropriate for a baby or toddler. As your child grows, the design of the room should grow with them. In this colorful little girl's room, the designer chose a simple desk and bookshelf with a white four-drawer chest. The square knobs on the dresser are hand painted in various colorful designs. The designer pulled from the kaleidoscope of color in the drawer knobs to choose the palette for the rest of the room—bright yellow walls, sage green chair, and plaid fabrics in the same color palette—to create a warm, happy environment. This is a design that can grow with the child, focused on accessories that can be easily changed, such as the fabric and playful knobs. The knobs on the dresser and desk can easily be replaced with solid color ones at a later time.

Design Details

Petite square knobs are handmade and decorated majolica with brass inserts and steel screws. The knobs are 1½" (3.8 cm) square with a 1¼" (3.2 cm) protrusion.

A child's room is a place to have fun with the design. Color, shape, and texture all come into play.

Home Work

When the homeowners, Garrison Hullinger and J. Jones, purchased this 1909 Foursquare in the suburbs, the house was in serious need of a makeover. The couple with contemporary taste purchased the property and set about making the space their own. One necessity was a home office. As with many telecommuting professionals today, a home office is a must-have in new and old floor plans alike. And these spaces need loads of storage to keep one organized. The homeowners introduced stained mahogany cabinetry that contrasts with the pale blue walls. The sizes of the pulls vary according to the size of the drawer they are installed on. For instance, they chose oversized stainless steel pulls on the largest drawer and a smaller version on the drawer for holding pens and pencils. The hinges are placed on the exterior of the cabinet doors to further accentuate the hardware's mechanism. Although a historical accent, the cupboard catches look truly contemporary against the dark wood. The exaggerated traditional forms are playful in a shiny finish and add personality to this otherwise serious working environment.

Design Details

The chrome hinge is placed on the exterior of the cabinet adding a decorative, bold touch to the office

The designer references the past in the bin pull—a ubiquitous fixture on 100-year-old cabinetry.

As the size and shape of the cubbyholes, drawers, and shelves are varied in size, so is the cabinet hardware—right down to the tiny chrome knob.

Popular at the turn of the twentieth century, the cupboard catch is introduced to this very contemporary cabinetry.

The home office, a common room in floor plans today, doesn't have to just be functional. Through its design details, it can be a place to add your personality.

Craftsman Living

For an architect to be well-versed in the vocabulary of a particular historical style takes skill and practice. To update that style for modern living takes ingenuity. For this exceptionally designed living space in a new bungalow in a suburban neighborhood, architect Dale Stewart took the details of the historical style while imposing modern living standards into the room. One of the tenets of Arts and Crafts design is the use of natural materials. Wood, stone, and metal work together to create a harmonious space. The details create well-appointed rooms. The natural, warm wood tones, box-beam ceiling, green ceramics, and built-in cabinetry all reflect the Craftsman style. The hand-hammered pulls on the cabinetry are in an antique copper patina. The cabinet door hardware in the same hand-hammered copper finish uses a ring pull rather than a bail pull. The hardware adds a decorative and functional touch to the flat-front drawers. The warm tone of the copper pulls melts into the honey tone of the wood. The cabinets hold DVDs for a flat-screen television tucked behind cabinetry on the opposite wall. Stewart has managed to blend the old and new into this new old house bungalow great room.

Design Details

The doors to the built-in cabinets have ring pulls paired with back plates in the same finish as the drawer pulls.

Architect Dale Stewart uses reproduction drawer pulls on his custom cabinetry. The design is reminiscent of hardware designed by Gustav Stickley in 1910. The bail pulls and back plates appear hand hammered in an antique copper finish.

The design of this living room speaks to the American Arts and Crafts movement, where simple forms and handcraft were revered.

Storage Spaces

Pantries, larders, and various other storage rooms come in all shapes and sizes and have a variety of cabinets, cupboards, and drawers in which to store items. And along with all these storage compartments comes the opportunity for lots of architectural hardware. Butler pantry drawers cry out for cup pulls, mudrooms would not be complete without pegs for coats and hats, and potting sheds would not function without cupboards with thumb catches for gardening tools.

Recognizing that storage is an important part of today's homes, architects and builders are putting these utilitarian rooms back into floor plans. The pantry is once again popular in new construction. Many designers look to the original space for design ideas. Glass-front cabinets with traditional cupboard catches and simple Victorian-era drawer pulls are among the most common choices for a traditional look. The mudroom is another area that has been reintroduced into housing construction. Rows of heavy-duty schoolhouse hooks and wooden pegs line the walls.

In these utilitarian spaces, the hardware is typically less decorative, although his-and-her closets can be highly stylized and dressed to the max including leather pulls on a handsome chest for him or dainty brass bail pulls for her. Anything goes! We'll look at how today's designers are treating these revived serviceable spaces and their hardware.

Storage areas can be found in all areas of the home. A hallway was fitted with bookcases to store books, tapes, photos, and DVDs. The drawer handles are decorative bird cage bail pulls.

Farmhouse Pantry

Modern necessity often betrays the simplicity of an authentic period-inspired room. At the 1843 home of architect Sandra Vitzthum, she sacrifices nothing in the design of her pantry—blending both function and aesthetic for this annexed kitchen space that reflects the home's past. Vitzthum has a sentimental connection to her home, known as the Loomis House. Her grandfather stayed in the house in 1938 while interviewing for a position as church minister and her grandmother lived next door to the property. Acting as steward to the house, Vitzthum wanted to incorporate a pantry into its original space just off the kitchen. To create a passageway between the kitchen and pantry, Vitzthum reconfigured the back steps. The pantry shelves are fashioned after a traditional dish pantry with glass-front doors trimmed with reproduction raw brass cupboard catches and bin pulls. It can take three to seven years to get that rich patina, but Vitzthum says it is worth the wait. (She has heard that you can accelerate the patina by placing them under a porch for a season. The exposure to air oxidizes the brass more quickly.) The center-mounted pulls contrast with the warm wood tones of the cabinets. Vitzthum likes the functionality of the pulls. She uses cupboard catches in cabinet designs because they help keep the door from warping.

Cupboard catches secure the dish cabinets and, as Vitzthum points out, help prevent the wood doors from warping.

Centered 3" (7.6 cm) bin pulls dress the flat-paneled drawers.

Vitzthum allowed the brass cupboard catches and bin pulls to oxidize naturally to create an aged patina.

Vintage Mudroom

Transformed into a galley kitchen in the 1950s, architect Sandra Vitzthum brought back the mudroom, or shed, to its original use—a common room attached to old farmhouses for people to change out of their outdoor clothes. She incorporated loads of storage into the space including a shelf that runs around the top of the room. It's lined with hockey skates, bike helmets, and football equipment. She also added vintage schoolhouse-style cast iron hooks for hats and coats. These early nineteenth-century spaces would originally have had pegs or nails on the wall for hanging clothes. On the opposite wall is a five-bay storage unit with ten cubbyholes—again with large cast iron hooks strong enough to hold her boys' winter gear. The walls are varnished pine bead board. Artisan Ruth Pope painted Green Mountain scenes on a hutch and chest for the shed outfitted with traditional bail pulls. The space is a cozy spot to don ski pants and winter gear before venturing out into the winter wonderland.

Design Details

The coat hooks are a turn-of-the-last-century schoolhouse style, which are sturdy enough for heavy winter coats.

Schoolhouse hooks were popular from the late 1800s through the 1940s in schoolhouses as well as other institutional buildings.

Personal Space

Although the design of this house makes reference to old-fashioned building traditions, its materials, details, and spatial organization make it a truly modern house. Architect Peter Rose is influenced in his work by many traditions, eras, and architects from the Shakers to Adolph Loos. In his design for this dressing room, the modern form comes to life in the fir wood custom-made cabinetry. Rose designed the pulls in nickel-plated steel and had them custom fabricated by a local craftsman. The hinges are concealed, adding to the clean lines in the room. Rose strives for a minimalist simplicity and clarity in his designs. He chose a lever handle for the door. He liked how it felt, looked, and worked. When incorporating hardware into the design of a home, he believes it is a personal choice.

Design Details

Rose further personalized the space by designing nickel-plated steel pulls. A local metalsmith fabricated the design.

The modern bronze lever handle in the bathroom is compliant with the American with Disabilities Act.

Architect Peter Rose created this dressing room based on his modern design philosophy.

Dressing Modern

Architect John Colamarino wanted to create a modern look in this client's dressing room. For the dressing table and cabinetry unit he chose oversized crescent chrome pulls. The doorknob is a simple contemporary ball also finished in chrome. Modern fixtures such as these came into the mass market in the early 1950s when modernism went mainstream. Designers, such as husband-and-wife team Charles and Ray Eames, brought modern forms into the forefront of house design. The pale blue, futuristic Morrow chair is a perfect fit for the modern space. The wire pulls play off the chrome legs with a bit of curve of their own. A vanity mirror is also finished in chrome and is perfectly appropriate for the ultramodern space. The design achieves its modern look with simplistic and sleek hardware details.

Design Details

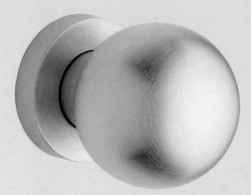

A simple ball doorknob in a chrome finish plays off the crescent pulls.

Sleek, elongated chrome-wire pulls with a slight curve accentuate the modern design of the space.

A refreshing approach to design, this dressing room is sleek, practical, and sophisticated.

Spelling Bee

Hardware comes in all shapes, sizes, and styles. And it is in this mudroom addition where the hardware shows a whimsical side. The homeowner needed easy access from the driveway to the kitchen, but wanted a transitional space where the kids could drop their bike gear, coats, muddy boots, and schoolbooks; Karen Morse of Karen Morse Construction gave her client all this and more. Because there are young children in the home, the homeowner wanted the space to be welcoming and playful. The coat hooks, which spell out their purpose, do just that. A simple gesture, but the design element creates personality in the small space. The bright white of the letters stands out against the red paint. The cubbyholes offer ample storage for shoes, bags, and bike helmets. The door has a sturdy thumb latch in a modified Craftsman style with a satin brass finish. It fits perfectly with the Arts and Crafts–style door.

Design Details

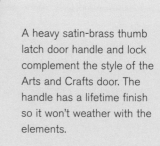

Clever coat hooks offer a playful alternative to traditional style in this new-construction mudroom.

A heavy satin-brass thumb latch door handle and lock complement the style of the Arts and Crafts door. The handle has a lifetime finish so it won't weather with the elements.

This mudroom is perfect for a family with young children.

Hooked on Design

Designer Connie Driscoll likes to have fun when she designs spaces. For this new home's sweet entryway, Driscoll incorporated traditional details with a twist. Bead board, crown molding, baseboards, and a decorative inset window mirror offer classic style while oversized, polished, chrome coat hooks add a playful approach to the space. We take ourselves too seriously these days, so it's great when you can add a dimension of fun to the design of even the smallest spaces. The giant coat hooks are replicas of the schoolhouse coat hook popular from the late 1800s to the 1940s in not only schoolhouses but homes as well. Driscoll turns up the design a notch—the hooks are not only sturdy and functional for hanging heavy winter coats, but they become a collection of art on the wall. The six hooks are unevenly spaced, which fills the blank wall with utility and style.

Design Details

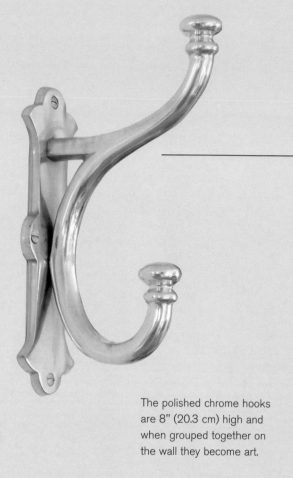

The polished chrome hooks are 8" (20.3 cm) high and when grouped together on the wall they become art.

Connie Driscoll thinks outside the box when it comes to her room designs —including this whimsical approach to a mudroom.

Swiss Contemporary

Swiss interior designer Sue Rohrer uses a bold mix of styles in her highly stylized spaces. She has turned an unspectacular old house near Zurich into a home full of color and life. Creating twenty-first-century spaces in the house was one of her goals. She transformed the square footage under the eaves into the homeowner's master suite including a bedroom, bath, and this wonderful dressing room. Hidden from the master bedroom behind a bookshelf, Rohrer designed built-in open shelving and cupboard spaces that follow the steep roofline. Rohrer designed a chest of drawers made-to-measure for the center of the space. For a masculine touch, Rohrer specified brown leather drawer pulls for the long drawers. A creative use of the sturdy material, the leather straps are the perfect complement to the space, offering texture and color to an otherwise simple composition.

Design Details

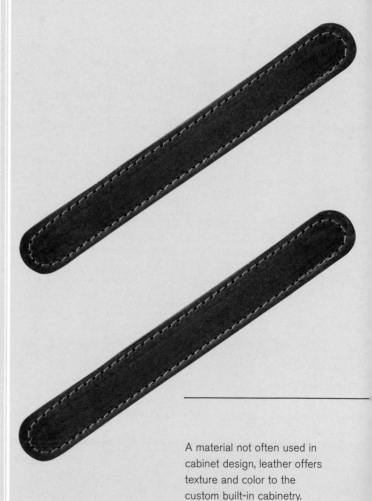

A material not often used in cabinet design, leather offers texture and color to the custom built-in cabinetry.

The custom closets in this Swiss farmhouse are ultracontemporary.

The Potting Shed

Another useful space in many older houses is the potting or cutting room. Used to repot plants for both indoor and outdoor use or to arrange flowers freshly cut from the garden into vases, this space is truly a gardener's delight. And what could be more appropriate in this utilitarian room than antique bead board cabinetry painted a crisp white? The iron cupboard catches on the cabinetry are the perfect accent to the piece. Simple bin pulls with a decorative pattern complete the look of the built-in cabinetry that stores all the accoutrements for attending the garden.

Design Details

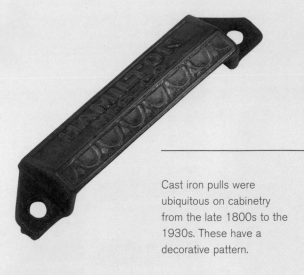

Cast iron pulls were ubiquitous on cabinetry from the late 1800s to the 1930s. These have a decorative pattern.

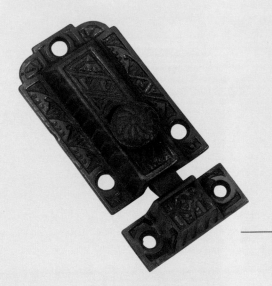

The cast iron cupboard catches have a decorative pattern that matches the pulls.

Often found in historical country houses of the rich, the potting or cutting room would offer ample storage for vases, pruning shears, and other garden implements. The choice of cast iron hardware was popular for such a room in the past and is popular again today.

Making an Entrance

Many homeowners share in the dilemma of how to make the exterior entrance to the home inviting and attractive. Not only does a handsome, well-designed entrance to your house say, "welcome", but it also creates that sought-after curb appeal.

To make your entry friendly, begin at your front door. Transform the front entryway into a focal point by installing a handsome and well-functioning door handle —it's the first thing many visitors to your home will touch. So get a good-quality lockset that leaves a solid first impression. There are many styles available on the marketplace, but remember to choose a lockset that is appropriate for your home's design. If you have a sweet bungalow, choose hardware that fits that architecture. For instance, a Craftsman-style back plate and door handle are perfect complements to the bungalow, but you certainly wouldn't want to choose a Federal-style brass doorknob or an Art Deco design. When choosing your house numbers, doorbell, and mailbox, one design approach is to choose the same finish and style as the doorknob. Also make sure that your house numbers are easily read from the street; you wouldn't want the pizza delivery guy to go to the wrong house on Super Bowl Sunday. And the mailbox should also be big enough to fit your September issue of *Vogue*!

But don't stop at the front door. Consider the design of your shutters, garage, and garden gate hardware. Does this exterior hardware work in harmony or does it lack continuity? We'll look at these outdoor spaces to determine which hardware works with which style.

This entryway to a Georgian townhouse in London represents the quintessential style of the eighteenth century. Georgian style lasted from the reign of King George I, who ascended the throne in 1711, until the American Revolution (King George III). Foundries in Birmingham churned out brass hardware to adorn such doors.

Medieval Manor

This new home designed by architect Sandra Vitzthum is reminiscent of an early twentieth-century carriage house. Built for Charlie Hayes, a sports car connoisseur, the house design appropriately has a pair of two-bay garages flanking the entryway. Another passion for Hayes is collecting both English and American Arts and Crafts antiques. To create a space that would reflect his large antiques collection, Vitzthum fashioned the house after the English Arts and Crafts style. Vitzthum was inspired by the father of the English Arts and Crafts movement, William Morris, as well as Philip Webb, Edwin Luytens, and C. F. A. Voysey. Vitzthum wanted the home's entryway to pay homage to these nineteenth-century tastemakers who shunned the gaudy factory-made goods of the Victorian era but embraced hand-crafts and celebrated natural and useful elements in the home. "It's all about the nature of the materials and the simplicity and clarity of intention," says Vitzthum, whose intention is clear in the entryway of the house. The simple door is a medieval form—board and batten in construction, made of cedar that has weathered over time. Ornamental flourishes come in the way of custom wrought iron strap hinges made by Lucien Avery. The scrolled iron hinge is paired with a simple thumb latch. The house is secured with a deadbolt installed above the thumb latch. The play of black wrought iron against the gray, weatherworn cedar creates a warm, welcoming entryway that celebrates the Arts and Crafts philosophy.

Design Details

Charlie Hayes found this antique doorknocker from the height of the Arts and Crafts era.

A traditional thumb latch in cast iron greets visitors.

The handcrafted strap hinges are inspired by a medieval English design.

This new house takes its inspiration from medieval forms, especially for its board and batten door and hand wrought strap hinges with decorative flourishes.

Country Retreat

While looking for a new home, architect John B. Murray stumbled upon this dilapidated Greek Revival farmhouse in the country. The 100-acre bucolic setting was ideal for a country retreat complete with views of the mountains, fields, and a lovely pond. However, the house had practically no redeeming qualities. Over the years, it had been stripped of all its original detailing—including its front door! To bring this front entryway back to its simple farmhouse charm, Murray found a reclaimed antique door from a salvage yard and painted it forest green, a color commonly used in the 1850s. Staying with salvaged materials, Murray added a brown porcelain knob, called a Bennington knob, to the home's front door. Porcelain knobs were common in houses built in the early 1800s. The Bennington knob, which is a bit more fanciful with its striated design, is the perfect way to dress the country door without going overboard. Although the doorknobs and roses are antique, Murray specified a new mortise lock for the door. Antique locks often have some of their parts missing and it can be difficult to find replacement pieces. The hand doorknocker is also an antique found at a local salvage yard. The knocker design is typical of the nineteenth-century Regency period and completes the entryway's design.

Design Details

There are a few reproduction Regency period doorknockers on the market today. The hand knocker swings from the back plate.

The brown porcelain Bennington knob was a popular choice for country houses in the mid-nineteenth century. Today, there are a few manufacturers reproducing the style.

John B. Murray found an old Greek Revival farmhouse that had lost most of its original features through the years. Murray scoured salvage yards to find the right historical elements—including the hardware—to restore the home.

Garden Gate

A garden gate marks the transition between the public and private areas of your home. It serves as both a frame to your home and as a property marker. Historically, a garden gate would keep wildlife from eating the tasty vegetables, herbs, and flowers inside. The garden gate and its hardware should be handsome, sturdy, functional, and reflect the style of the home. A grand home might have a grand iron gate, while a country cottage will have a simple picket fence. At this country retreat house renovation, architect John B. Murray chose a historically appropriate gate for the mid-nineteenth-century home. It's an early nineteenth-century American vernacular with reproduction hardware fashioned after hardware found at Colonial Williamsburg. The hand-wrought hardware includes a latch strap, hinges, and a cannonball counterweight gate closer. The weight of the replica Civil War–style cast iron gate closer slowly pulls the gate shut. The hardware is coated with a protective coating that will protect it from the elements for years to come. A garden gate is the first impression one receives when entering a home and is a way to add artistic expression to the home. If done well, its hardware should complement the design.

Design Details

Although Murray designed the gate hardware and had it forged by a local blacksmith, there are several hardware companies that carry historically appropriate stock pieces.

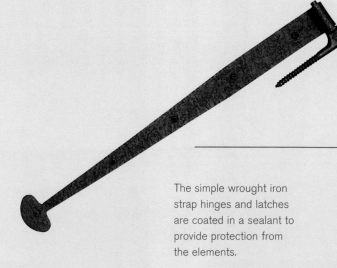

The simple wrought iron strap hinges and latches are coated in a sealant to provide protection from the elements.

Murray designed a garden gate and its hardware to reflect the nineteenth-century origins of this country farmhouse.

Delightful Doors

After searching for years for an old Greek Revival house to fix up as a weekend retreat, architect Gil Schafer fell in love with a rolling piece of property and decided to design his own Greek Revival home to fit in with the antique house styles of the area. Before sitting down at the drafting board, Schafer studied many old Greek Revivals as well as historical builders' pattern books. Once he had studied every aspect of the design, he was ready to create his dream home. "It's about immersing yourself in the details and developing a fluency in the language of the style. You aren't copying your sources but your work is deeply informed by them," says Schafer. This is especially true of design choices in the home such as the entryway to the back gardens. An original upstate Greek Revival house would not have been built with French doors leading out into a formal garden, but one can easily imagine these doors as a later twentieth-century addition to such a structure. The three-paned doors are outfitted with delicate solid-cast brass lever handles and brass roses. The levers, which have universal handing, also speak of a later era. The door has full-mortise butt hinges with a ball finial finished in antiqued brass. A narrow backset mortise lock and slide bolt at both the top and bottom of the doorframes secure the doors. The outcome is a refined and enchanting entryway to a back terrace that, although not strictly Greek Revival, enhances the historical style.

Design Details

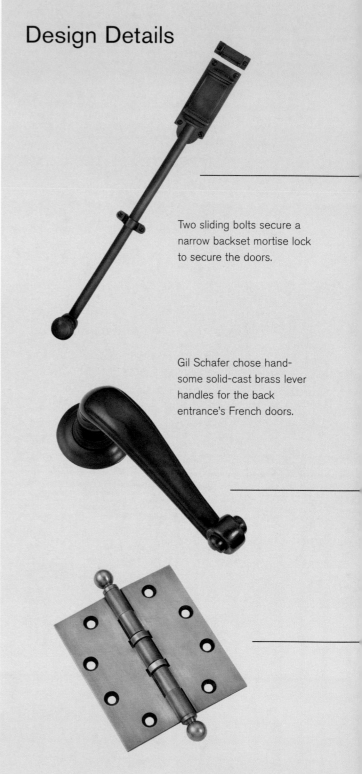

Two sliding bolts secure a narrow backset mortise lock to secure the doors.

Gil Schafer chose handsome solid-cast brass lever handles for the back entrance's French doors.

Three hinges, also finished in antique brass, allow for movement.

Although not found on original Greek Revival homes, the French doors on architect Gil Schafer's country retreat add grace and beauty to the space. The architectural hardware complements the design.

Arts and Crafts Entry

When architect Dale Stewart, of Core Architecture, purchased a small lot in a well-established suburban neighborhood, he wanted to design a house that would fit in contextually. The challenge was to arrange the house so its mass did not overpower the other houses on the street, which included smaller ones and one-and-a-half story Tudor-, Cape Cod-, bungalow-, and ranch-style homes. The final result is a welcoming 3,400-square-foot (316 sq m) bungalow-style, two-level home with a warm, inviting wraparound porch. The entryway is a handsome Craftsman-style door. The hardware chosen for the entryway is durable, inspired by the early Arts and Crafts movement, and echoes the theme of the architecture. An oversized copper mailbox with Craftsman-style flourishes, copper house numbers in a period-appropriate style, and a doorbell plate with a rectilinear grid pattern all complement the entryway's antiqued bronze thumb latch. Stewart has held the design theme together through the use of accessories. In the true Arts and Crafts tradition, these accessories appear to be hand forged in materials used by early craftsman artisans: copper, brass, and bronze. The detailing is true to the early Craftsman designs made popular by leaders of the early movement such as American designer Gustav Stickley. He believed that the simplicity of Craftsman architecture made the details an important part of the overall design. Stewart takes this design philosophy to heart in the design of this entryway.

Design Details

The doorbell plate matches the handset and is also a quintessential Craftsman form.

The house numbers, in traditional Craftsman style, are easy to read from the street.

The copper mailbox is pressed copper with a relief of a naturalistic scene—a popular motif in the American Arts and Crafts genre.

The entryway lockset is a traditional Craftsman-style thumb latch.

Architect Dale Stewart created a cozy bungalow for his young family. He carried the bungalow theme to the hardware—including a copper mailbox complete with a naturalistic scene.

Dutch Doors

Architect Bernard Wharton of Shope, Reno, and Wharton designed a Shingle-style house with Colonial Revival details. The warm, welcoming entryway features a mahogany Dutch door. In typical Netherlands style, the Colonial Dutch-American exterior doors split horizontally in the center so the upper section could be opened independently of the lower half to let in light and fresh air while keeping children in and wildlife out. Wharton added a solid brass rim lock to the door, a lock found on many eighteenth-century homes. This type of lock was typically made in English brass foundries and imported into America in the 1700s and 1800s. This particular rim lock is a reproduction. The door's top has twelve panes and is secured in the closed position with two slide bolts or is held open with a hook that is secured to the wall. The finish on all the hardware is an antiqued brass. To protect against the coastal elements, the exterior is finished with a PVD coating. The interior mellows with age as it is handled over time.

Design Details

The hooks are also solid brass and, like the rest of the hardware, are left unfinished so they will acquire patina.

The reproduction rim lock, one of the oldest types of locks dating back to the mid-1700s, is a perfect addition to the Colonial Revival style.

Shope, Reno, and Wharton adds interest to the front door with its brass hardware accessories.

West Indies Inspiration

When architect Eric Watson set out to design his contemporary house, he drew upon Old World styles for inspiration. The houses he had seen in the Dutch West Indies heavily influenced Watson. The home is based on historical antecedents—a combination of Dutch Colonial, French Colonial, and mission styles. Walls and double doors with grilled panels enclose the front courtyard and entrance to the property. The shutters on the parapet wall are borrowed from a house Watson saw on Curacao, a Dutch island. The lever handle on the entry door to the courtyard is simple wrought iron—an appropriate choice for a house inspired by early Colonial designs. The house numbers are large in an antique serif typeface and are in wrought iron as well. The operable shutters are held open with wrought iron shutter dogs in the shape of the letter S. To protect against the sea air, the hardware is finished with a PVD coating. Simple Colonial touches punctuate the eclectic Old World styles found throughout the house.

Design Details

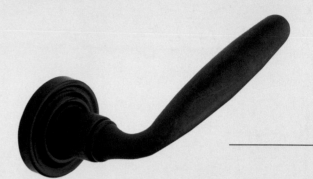

The lever has an oil-rubbed bronze finish.

The diamond-motif shutters are held open with wrought iron shutter dogs, a popular design style since the early 1700s.

Eric Watson took inspiration from a number of Colonial styles including Dutch, French, and Mission. The home's hardware is rustic and simple.

Glossary of Hardware Terms

A

ACTIVE DOOR: In a pair of doors, the active door is the one that must be opened first.

A. D. A. (Americans with Disabilities Act): An act to establish a clear and comprehensive prohibition of discrimination on the basis of disability.

ADJUSTABLE KEY: A key for sliding door locks that has a stem or shank that adjusts its length according to the various thicknesses of the doors.

ANTIFRICTION BOLT: The latch bolt of a lock with a device for diminishing the sliding friction of the bolt during the closing of a door. A small additional latch connected with a regular latch bolt. It engages the strike and retracts the regular latch.

ASTRAGAL: A molding, usually half round, applied to the abutting edges of a pair of double or folding doors to break and cover the line of juncture or act as a stop.

ASTRAGAL FRONT: A lock front of a form coinciding in shape with the edges of a door having an astragal molding.

AUXILIARY LATCH BOLT (GUARD LATCH): A latch bolt separate from the regular latch bolt that remains retracted when the door is closed and automatically dead locks the regular latch against end pressure.

AUXILIARY SPRING: A device applied under a rose to hold a lever handle in a horizontal position.

B

BACK PLATE (RIM CYLINDER): A small plate applied to the inside of the door through which the cylinder's connecting screws are passed.

BACKSET OF A LOCK: The distance horizontally from the front to the center of the knob or keyhole.

BALL BEARING BUTT: A butt having a roller or ball bearing to reduce the friction.

BAR HANDLE: A door handle consisting of a bar, usually horizontal, supported by one or more projecting brackets.

BARN DOOR LATCH: A heavy thumb latch.

BARREL BOLT: A cylindrical bolt mounted on a plate that has a case projecting from its surface to contain and guide the bolt.

BARREL KEY: A round key that has a hole drilled into its end to fit over a drill pin in the lock. Used chiefly for cabinet locks, synonymous with pipe key.

BEVEL OF BOLT: A term used to indicate the direction in which the bevel of the latch bolt is inclined; regular bevel commonly indicating a lock for use on a door opening inward and reverse bevel for a door opening outward.

BEVEL OF DOOR: The angle made by the edge of a door with the sides of the lock stile, if other than 90 degrees.

BEVEL OF LOCK FRONT: The angle of the front of a mortise lock, when inclined at other than a right (90 degree) angle to the case, to conform to the angle of the edge of the door.

BIT (OF A KEY): A projecting blade that engages with and actuates either or both the bolt and tumblers of the lock. The part of a key that is cut to operate a lock.

BIT-KEY LOCK: A lock operated by a key that has a wing bit.

BITTING: A cut or indentation on that part of a key that acts upon and sets the tumblers.

BOLT: A bar or barrier arranged to secure a door or other moving part and to prevent its opening.

BOLT (NECKED): A bolt, the projecting end of which has a bend or offset to engage with a strike or keeper not in line with the body of the bolt.

BOTTOM BOLT: A general term defining any bolt specifically designed for use only on the bottom of a door.

BOW: The portion of the key that is held between the fingers.

BOX STRIKE: A strike on which the aperture to receive the bolt is enclosed or boxed.

BRACKET BEARING: A knob thimble, or socket that projects like a bracket, supporting the knob close to its head instead of at the end of the shank.

BUILDERS' FINISHING HARDWARE: (Also architectural hardware) A term to designate the locks, hinges, and other metallic trimmings used on buildings for protective and decorative purposes; as distinguished from rough hardware, which includes such building items as nails, registers, ash pit doors, stanchions, sash weights, sash cords, sash chains, and pulleys.

BUTT: An abbreviation of the term butt hinge. A hinge intended for application to the butt or edge of a door, in contrast to a flat or strap hinge for application to the surface of a door.

BUTT (HALF SURFACE): A butt with one leaf mortised in frame, the other applied on the surface of the door.

C

CABINET LOCK: A small cylinder, bit, or flat key lock used on cabinetwork or furniture.

CARD PLATE: A holder used on drawers or doors formed to hold a label or card.

CAM: A rotating piece, either noncircular or concentric, used to convert rotary into reciprocating motion; e.g., the wing of a bit key or a cylinder cam that converts rotary into reciprocal motion when actuating the bolts of a lock.

CAM (OF A CYLINDER): A rotating piece attached to the end of the cylinder plug to operate the locking mechanism.

CAP (OF A LOCK): The removable lid of a lock case.

CAPPED BUTT: A butt having on each leaf a cap that covers the fastening screws and is itself attached to the butt by one or more smaller screws.

CASEMENT ADJUSTER: A fringed or pivoted rod for moving and fastening the hinged sash of a casement or French window.

CASEMENT FASTENER: A catch for fastening a casement or French window.

CASEMENT WINDOW: A window (sash) hinged at the sides to open horizontally in or out.

CATCH: A flat metal fitting applied to the doorjamb designed to catch the latch of a thumb latch as it falls.

CHAIN BOLT: A bolt for application at the top of a door to retract against the resistance of a spring, which tends to hold it in the locked position.

CHAIN DOOR FASTENER: A heavy chain, one end of which is secured to a plate that may be attached to the edge of the door, the other end of which has a ball or hook that may be inserted in a slot formed in another plate attached to the jam or other half of the door; it prevents the door from being opened (except slightly) until the chain is released.

CHANGE KEY: A key that will operate only one lock in a series, as distinguished from a master key that will operate all locks in a series.

CHANGES (KEY): The different bittings or tumbler arrangements in a series.

CITY LOCK: (1904 Towne usage) A nearly obsolete term used in New York City and vicinity; formerly indicated a superior grade of handmade locks, but now usually applied to an inferior grade of rim and mortise locks with brass bolts and steel or brass keys.

CLOSET KNOB: A single knob on one end of a spindle, on the other end of which is a rose or plate to secure the knob and spindle to the door; for use on closet doors. Also called a dummy knob.

COAT AND HAT HOOK: A hook with two or more projections, one of which is of sufficient length to receive a hat, the others being usually shorter.

COMBINATION LOCK: A lock having changeable tumblers actuated by a dial on the face of a door that is permanently connected by a spindle with the lock mechanism.

COMBINED ESCUTCHEON PLATE: A plate containing both a keyhole and a knob rose.

COMMUNICATING DOOR LOCK: A lock that usually has a latch bolt and two dead bolts; one dead bolt is controlled by a turn knob or key from one side only and the other dead bolt is controlled from the opposite side only, each independently of the other.

COMPENSATING-HUB: A lock hub that has an elongated spindle hole to compensate for the shrinking and swelling of a door and to prevent derangement of the lock and binding due to other causes.

CORNER PLATE: A plate similar to a finger or push plate but with two arms that form a right angle, making it appropriate for applying to the corner of a door.

COTTAGE LATCH: A small lift latch for use on cupboards and light doors.

CRANK HANDLE: Synonymous with lever handle.

CREMONE BOLT: A fastening that is applied to the surface of casement or French windows consisting of a sliding rod that engages the window frame at the top and bottom with strikes or plates and has a handle or knob positioned near the center; the rotation of the knob or handle causes the upper and lower parts of the bolt to move in opposite directions for locking or unlocking; it sometimes has an additional horizontal bolt that operates simultaneously to further to secure the sash at or near its center.

CUP ESCUTCHEON: A doorplate used on sliding doors that have a recessed panel that creates a finger hold and contains the knob (or its equivalent) and a key; all of the contained parts are flush with the surface of the plate to not obstruct the movement of the door within its recess.

CUPBOARD BUTTON: A small turning bar adapted to secure a door.

CUPBOARD CATCH: A small spring catch adapted for fastening a light door and operated by a slide knob or thumb piece.

CUPBOARD LOCK: A lock designed for use on doors of cupboards, boxes, and so forth.

CUPBOARD TURN: A small spring-catch adapted for fastening a light door and operated by rotating a knob or handle.

CURVED LIP STRIKE: The lip of a strike curved to conform to a detail in order to protect door casings and to prevent the catching of wearing apparel on the projecting lip.

CYLINDER (OF A LOCK): A cylindrically shaped device containing the key-controlled mechanism and cam or spindle for actuating the bolts of a lock.

CYLINDER LOCK: A lock that has a removable tumbler assembly contained in a cylindrical case.

CYLINDER COLLAR: A decorative plate placed under the head of a cylinder to give a finished appearance.

CYLINDER RING: A rose or washer placed under the head of a cylinder to permit the use of a long or standard cylinder on a thin door.

CYLINDER SCREW: The setscrew in the front of a mortise lock to prevent the unscrewing of a cylinder.

CYLINDRICAL: A term used to describe locks with a cylindrical case that has a separate latch bolt case that fits into the cylindrical lock case.

D

DEAD BOLT (OF A LOCK): The projecting member of a lock that is operated by key or turn-knob to positively lock a door; is usually rectangular.

DEAD LOCK: A lock with a dead bolt only, controlled by a key from either side or by a key on one side and a turn knob on the other side.

DISCTUMBLER: A flat, circular, or oval disc with a rectangular hole and one or more side projections. A number of them are used side-by-side.

DOOR BOLT: A sliding rod or bar suitably mounted for attaching to a door and to secure it.

DOOR CHECK: A device for to prevent doors with springs from slamming, synonymous with door check and spring.

DOOR CHECK AND SPRING: A device combining, in one mechanism, a door spring and a check to prevent the door from slamming.

DOOR CLOSER BRACKET: A device that allows a door closer to be installed on the stop or push side of a door. Brackets are of several different types for various applications.

DOOR HOLDER: A device for holding a door in an open position.

DOOR STOP: A device that limits the swing of a door that is generally applied to the floor or wall base.

DOUBLE-ACTING SPRING HINGE: A device for hanging a door that allows the door to swing in either direction. Additionally, the hinge has two springs that return the door from either an open position or the closed.

DOUBLE-HUNG WINDOW (SASH): A window with two vertical sashes that slide up and down.

DOUBLE-THROW BOLT: A bolt controlled by a mechanism that permits extra projection or throw of the bolt, giving greater security.

DRAW BACK BOLT: A bolt (or slide) whose handle or curved shape extends from the side of the lock case opposite the face. When drawn, it retracts the latch.

DRAW BACK LOCK: A lock that has a latch operated from the inside by a draw back bolt that extends from the side of the case opposite the face. May or may not have a stop to hold the latch against the key that operates the lock from the outside.

DRAWER KNOB: A small knob used for pulling open a drawer.

DRAWER PULL: A small handle or grip used similarly to a drawer knob.

DRILL PIN: A round pin projecting from the back plate of a lock that fits into a hole in the end of the key.

DROP DRAWER PULL: A pull or handle that pivots at the ends of its attaching plate.

DROP ESCUTCHEON (OR KEY PLATE): An escutcheon that has a pivoted covering for the keyhole.

DUMMY CYLINDER: An inactive cylinder that attaches to a cylinder collar or escutcheon for use as dummy trim.

DUMMY TRIM: Trim only, without a lock or working parts that may be applied to the inactive door of a pair of doors and matches the trim on the active door. This is used to balance the hardware ornamentation on a pair of doors.

DUTCH DOOR: A door cut horizontally through the lock rail so that the upper part of the door may be opened independently of the lower door.

DUTCH DOOR BOLT: A bolt for locking together the upper and lower halves of a Dutch door.

E

ELBOW CATCH: A catch with a pivoted L-shaped member one end of which engages a strike or staple and the other end forms a handle to release the catch.

ESCUTCHEON: A plate containing a keyhole.

ESCUTCHEON PLATE: A protective metal plate applied to the surface of the lock stile with or without a cylinder hold or keyhole but with a knob socket.

ESCUTCHEON KNOB: A doorknob containing a keyhole for the key that actuates the lock or controls the rotation of the knob.

ESPAGNOLETTE BOLT (BAR): A fastening applied to the surface of French windows (doors) or casement windows. Consists of rotating rods that extend from the top to the bottom with hooks at each end. When the bar rotates, the hooks on the rods engage with the pins or plates in the window frames. The bar has a hinged handle near the center that may be rotated to fasten or release the sash.

EXTENSION BOLT: A flush bolt that has a short plate to receive a knob or thumb piece, of which the latter is connected at the bolt end at the top or bottom of a door by an extension rod inserted through a hole bored through the door's thickness.

F

FACE (OF A LOCK): The plate surface that shows at the edge of the door after installation.

FAST PIN JOINT BUTT: A butt in which the pin is permanently fastened.

FENCE (OF A LOCK): A projecting piece usually attached to the tail of the dead bolt that passes through the gating of the lever tumblers when they are property aligned, permitting the bolt to be projected or retracted.

FINISHING HARDWARE: Hardware that may be considered part of the decorative or finished treatment of a room or building.

FLUSH BOLT: A door bolt designed so that when applied, the surface is flush with the door.

FLUSH CUPBOARD CATCH: A catch that is half mortise, i.e., flush with the face of the door.

FLUSH PLATE: A doorplate of any kind intended to be set into the wood flush with its surface.

FLUSH RING: A flush circular door pull that is mortised into the door.

FLUSH RING CUPBOARD CATCH: A catch with a flush ring in place of a knob for actuating the bolt.

FRENCH DOOR: A full-length glass-paned door, sometimes called a French window or a sash door.

FRENCH ESCUTCHEON: A small circular key plate secured by driving or screwing into the wood.

FRENCH SHANK: A term used to indicate an ornamentally shaped knob shank.

FRENCH WINDOW: A window mounted on hinges like a door; a casement window extending to the floor.

FRENCH WINDOW LOCK: A mortise knob lock with a narrow backset for use on French windows or doors with narrow stiles.

FRONT (OF A LOCK): The faceplate of a mortise lock through which the ends of the bolts are projected.

FRONT DOOR LOCK: A lock used on entrance doors that has a dead bolt and a latch bolt; the former is controlled from the outside by a key and from the inside by a key or knob, and the latter is controlled from the outside by a key and from the inside by a knob. Usually provided with a stop work that allows the outside knob to be set to actuate the latch bolt or not, as desired.

G

GRILLE: A protective screen of open metalwork made of either wrought or cast iron; sometimes highly ornamental.

H

HAND AND BEVEL OF LOCKS: The inclination or bevel of the latch bolt and the lock front always correspond to the direction of the bevel of the door. If no bevel is designated, it is understood to be a regular bevel. The hand of such a lock is the same as the hand of the door.

HANDRAIL BRACKET: A support for stair handrails.

HAND (OF LOCKS): A term indicating whether the hardware is adaptable for use on a right- or left-hand door.

HANDED: A term indicating that the hardware is adaptable for use on either a right-hand or left-hand door, but not both.

H-HINGE: A type of strap hinge with enlarged leaves so that when the hinge is open, it forms the letter H; also known as a parliament hinge or a shutter hinge.

HARMON HINGE: A hinge designed to swing a door into a pocket at a right angle with the frame.

HINGED OR SWINGING LATCH BOLT: A bolt that is hinged to the lock front and is retracted with a swinging rather than a sliding action.

HORIZONTAL LOCK: A lock whose major dimension is horizontal.

J

JAMB: The inside vertical face of a door or window frame.

K

KEY ESCUTCHEON: A small plate with a keyhole only.

KEYHOLE: The aperture in a lock case or escutcheon plate through which the key passes when entering the lock. *Also see* key way.

KEY PLATE: A plain or ornamental plate that has a keyhole (but no knob socket) to be attached to the surface of a door.

KEY WAY: The aperture throughout the length of a lock cylinder into which the key is inserted.

KICK PLATE: A plate applied near the bottom of the door to protect the surface.

KNOB: A projecting handle, usually round or spherical, that operates a latch bolt. A small crescent- or otherwise-shaped knob designed to be operated by fingers is called a turn knob or sometimes a thumb turn or thumb knob that is usually employed to throw the dead bolt of a lock from the inside.

KNOB BOLT: A dead bolt that is controlled by a knob from either or both sides of the door and not actuated by a key.

KNOB LATCH: A door latch that has a spring bolt only and is operated by knobs.

KNOB LOCK: A door lock that has a spring latch operated by knobs and a dead bolt.

KNOB ROSE: A small plate that acts as a knob bearing and as a protective or ornamental shield applied to the surface of a door.

KNOB SCREW: A set (or other) screw to fasten a knob to a spindle.

KNOB SHANK: The projecting stem of a knob that contains the hole or socket that receives the spindle.

KNOB TOP: The larger upper part of a knob that is grasped by the hand.

KNUCKLE: The part of a hinge or butt that encloses the hinge pin.

L

LATCH: A door-fastening device that has a spring bolt but usually does not lock.

LATCH BOLT (OF A LOCK): A beveled spring bolt that is usually operated by knob, lever handle, or thumb piece.

LETTER BOX BACK PLATE: A plate attached to the inside of the door that finishes off the opening of the letter drop.

LETTER BOX HOOD: A cover to conceal the opening and to direct the mail towards the floor.

LETTER BOX PLATE: A cast or wrought iron plate attached to the door with an opening to permit insertion of mail.

LEVER CUPBOARD CATCH: A catch consisting of a lever pivoted on a plate through which it passes; its inner end is a hook that engages with a staple; its other end is in the shape of a knot or handle.

LEVER HANDLE: A horizontal handle for operating the latch bolt of a lock.

LEVER TUMBLER LOCK: Also called bit-key lock.

LOCK (INVERTED): A lock with the keyhole located above the knot or handle.

LOCK STILE (OF A DOOR): The stile to which the lock is applied, as distinguished from the hinged stile.

LOCKER RING: A pull that is mortised into the edge of a sliding locker door, which consists of a plate containing a ring that may be pushed back flush with the plate or pulled forward for use as a pull to open the door.

M

MORTISE: An opening made to receive a lock or other hardware; also the act of making such an opening.

MORTISE BOLT: A door bolt designed to be mortised into a door instead of being applied to its surface.

MORTISE LOCK OR LATCH: A lock or latch designed to be mortised into the edge of a door, not applied to the surface.

MUNTINS: The small members, either vertical or horizontal, that divide a glass door, or windows.

N

NONFERROUS: Nonrusting, does not contain iron.

O

OLIVE KNUCKLE HINGE: A paumelle hinge with knuckles arranged in an oval shape.

OUTSIDE: Term used to indicate the side from which the hand and bevel of locks are determined, usually the outside of an entrance door, the hall side of a room door, and the room side of a closet door. It is less confusing to determine the hand and bevel of a lock from the side that has the more important key function or, if the key function is the same on both sides, from the side on which the butts are visible.

P

PARLIAMENT BUTT: A butt that has T-headed, usually broad leaves.

PIN TUMBLERS: Small sliding pins in a lock cylinder that work against coil springs and prevent the cylinder plug from rotating until it is raised to an exact height by bitting the key.

PLATE ESCUTCHEON: Synonymous with key plate.

PULL BAR: A bar attached to a door in contradistinction to a push bar.

PULL-DOWN HANDLE: A light handle for attaching to the underside of the bottom rail of tipper sashes in order to move them.

PULL-DOWN HOOK: Synonymous with sash hook.

PULLEY STILE: The vertical sides of a double-hung sash casing to which the pulleys are applied.

R

RABBET: The offset on the abutting edge of a pair of doors or the corresponding offset of the fronts and strikes of rabbeted locks.

RABBETED LOCK: A lock in which the front is formed in two planes or steps corresponding to the rabbeted edge of the door.

RAIL (OF A DOOR): Any of the horizontal members that enclose the panels and that with the stiles constitute the framework.

REVERSE BEVEL (OF A LATCH BOLT): A term used to indicate that the bevel of the latch bolt is reversed or inclined in a direction opposite to the norm.

REVERSED DOOR: A door that opens in a direction opposite to the norm. Doors to rooms generally open inward. If they open outward, they are called reversed. Cupboard doors regularly open out.

RIM LOCK OR LATCH: A lock or latch that is applied to the surface of the door, not mortised into it.

ROSE: A small plate that acts as a knob bearing with sockets of varying depth for supporting and guiding the shank of a knob or lever.

ROSE (AUXILIARY): A rose equipped with a spring on the underside to hold a lever handle in a horizontal position.

ROUND KEY: A key that has a round shank or stem.

S

SASH LOCK: A fastening controlled by a key and used to secure a sash.

SASH PIN: A form of window spring bolt.

SASH PULL: A handle that attaches to the underside of the lower rail of an upper sash of a double-hung window for pulling down the sash. Synonymous with window pull down or pull-down handle.

SASH RIBBON: A thin metal band used with sliding sashes in place of a cord or rope.

SASH WEIGHT: A weight used to balance sliding sashes; usually made of cast iron and in a long, cylindrical shape.

STRAP HINGE: A surface-mounted hinge with long flaps of metal on each side that are secured to a door and adjacent post or wall.

STRIKE: A metal fastening on the door frame into which the bolt or lock is projected to secure the door. Applied both to the flat plate used with mortise locks and to the projecting box used with rim locks. Synonymous with striker, striking plate, and keeper.

T

TAIL PIECE: The sliding part or connecting link through which the bolt is operated by hub or key.

THUMB BOLT: A door bolt operated by a rotating thumb piece or a small knob.

THUMB LATCH: A door fastening consisting of a pivoted bar that crosses the joint of the door to engage with the strike on the jamb; the free end of the bar is raised by a transverse pivoted bar passing through the door that disengages it from the strike on the jamb; the latter bar is operated on one side by the thumb and on the other side by a finger.

THUMB PIECE: A stationary knob that usually operates independently from the locking device.

TUBULAR LOCK: A type of bored lock in which the bolt is enclosed in a tube.

Resources

Acorn Forged Iron
Early American hardware—Supplier of brass and iron hardware for exterior and interior doors, cabinet and shutter hardware, bath and fireplace accessories; mailboxes.
Web: www.acornmfg.com
Phone: 800.835.0121

Al Bar-Wilmette Platers
Hardware restoration—Restorer of old door and window hardware: repairs, cleans, polishes, and replates hardware and other metalwork of all finishes.
Web: www.albarwilmette.com
Phone: 866.823.8404

Antique Hardware and Home
Searches the globe for useful and interesting products and brings them to you at the lowest possible prices. Products run the gamut from cabinet hardware to telephone booths and from rubber duckies to magnificent claw-foot bathtubs.
Web: www.antiquehardware.com
Phone: 800.422.9982

Architectural Ironmongery Ltd.
Restoration hardware—Hardware, security, bathroom, and electrical fittings; doorknobs, window fixtures; hardware for old house restoration as well as construction of new homes.
Web: www.arciron.com
Phone: +44 0.1989.567946

Architectural Resource Center
Builder's hardware—Supplier of door, window, cabinet, and millwork hardware; window pulleys; cast bronze, brass, and aluminum.
Web: www.aresource.com
Phone: 800.370.8808

Architectural Windows and Entries
Windows and entry systems—Manufacturer of windows, doors, and entry systems: solid timber; residential, and commercial projects; custom made.
Web: www.architecturalwindows.com
Phone: 800.747.6840

Artifaqt
Architectural hardware accessories—Decorative switch plates.
Web: www.artifaqt.com
Phone: 610.935.0920

Artistic Doors and Windows
Stock and custom doors and windows—Manufacturer of hardwood doors and windows: traditional and contemporary styles; hardware.
Web: www.artisticdoorsandwindows.com
Phone: 732.726.9400

Atlas Homewares
Hardware—Contemporary hardware for the home.
Web: www.atlanshomewares.com
Phone: 818.240.3500

Baldwin
Brass hardware—Doorknobs, bathroom fixtures, knockers, lampposts, bath suites, interior lighting.
Web: www.baldwinhardware.com
Phone: 800.566.1986

Ball and Ball Hardware
Authentic restoration hardware—Supplier of authentic eighteenth- and nineteenth-century hardware: hinges, latches, pulls, shutter hardware, and more; custom work and repairs.
Web: www.ballandball-us.com
Phone: 800.257.3711

Baltica
Handcrafted hardware—Supplier of hardware: unique door and cabinet hardware, cremones, hinge finials, and switch plates; made in Europe.
Web: www.baltica.com
Phone: 866.699.3140

Bauerware
Cabinet hardware—Knobs, pulls, bathroom cabinets, cabinets in general, contemporary cabinets, children's cabinets, traditional cabinets, vintage cabinetware.
Web: www.bauerware.com
Phone: 415.864.3889

Beech River Mill
Custom shutters—Custom fabricator of exterior and interior shutters: paneled and louvered; duplication of any shutter using original nineteenth-century machinery; antique shutter hardware.
Web: www.beechrivermill.com
Phone: 603.539.2636

Blum
Cabinets—Hinges, drawer runners, specialty hardware, connectors.
Web: www.blum.com
Phone: +43.5578.7050

Bovard Studio, Inc.
Stained and beveled glass doors—Designer and manufacturer of glass doors: many designs, colors and textures; twenty-five styles and sizes with round top or rectangular frames; insulated-glass options.
Web: www.bovardstudio.com
Phone: 641.472.2824

BrassArt
Heritage brass—doorknobs, lighting fixtures, and wall design are some of the things found at BrassArt, one of the only brass-making companies left in the UK.
Web: www.brassart.co.uk
Phone: +44 0.1922.740512

Bronze Craft Corp.
Bronze hardware—Foundry: stock and custom architectural hardware for windows and doors; various metals.
Web: www.bronzecraft.com
Phone: 800.488.7747

Carl Martinez Hardware
Fixtures—Lighting, doorknobs, furniture, curtain fixtures, cabinet pulls, candle holders.
Web: www.carlmartinezhardware.com
Phone: 212.941.8142

Cifial
Brass hardware—Produces decorative brass products including locks, door hardware, faucets, custom shower components, bath accessories, and related products.
Web: www.cifialusa.com
Web: www.cifial.co.uk
Phone: 800.528.4904

Conquest Architectural Ironmongery
Door and window furnishings—Solid brass, solid bronze, and black malleable materials; periods vary from Louis XIV to Art Deco.
Web: www.conquestai.co.uk/doorfurniture.htm
Phone: +44 0.1424.777873

Courtyard Accessories
Antique/Modern—British-based hardware company featuring antique-styled furnishings such as doorknobs and locks, as well as more modern style furnishings such as shelving units and cabinets.
Web: US/CAN: www.courtyard-accessories.com/acatalog/index.html
Web: UK: www.courtyard-accessories.co.uk/online_shop.html
Phone: +44 0.1564.792312

Craftsmen Hardware Co.
Arts and Crafts—style hardware—Supplier of hardware: door, window, cabinet and drapery hardware and more; hand-hammered copper.
Web: www.craftsmenhardware.com
Phone: 660.376.2481

Crown City Hardware Co.
Historic hardware—Manufacturer of door, window, cabinet, transom and specialty hardware: Victorian, Arts and Crafts, Colonial, Art Deco, and other styles.
Web: www.crown-city.com
Phone Pasadena: 626.794.1188
Phone (Catalog Direct): 626.794.0234

Custom Trades International, Inc.
Doors and windows—Manufacturer of wood doors and shutters, wood and metal windows: oak, mahogany, and teak; hand-crafted hardware, primarily for European-style windows and doors in bronze and brass.
Web: www.customtrades.com
Phone: 203.561.5915

Emtek
Architectural hardware—handle sets, cabinet hardware
Web: www.emtek.com
Phone: 800.356.2741

E. R. Butler & Co.
Fine architectural hardware—Manufacturer of door hardware, bath fittings, cabinet and furniture mounts, lighting, and more: all metals; all period styles.
Web: www.erbutler.com
Phone Boston: 617.722.0230
Phone New York: 212.925.3565

European Hardware and Finishes/Gerber Hinge
Hardware—Supplier of locks, hinges, esculcheons, pulls, pendants, and decorative nails.
Web: www.gerber-hinge.com
Phone: 800.643.7237

Expo Design Center
A Home Depot company—Small appliances, outdoor living, decorative accessories, lighting and fans, kitchens, baths, door locks and hard-ware, indoor living, custom designs.
Web: www.expo.com
Phone: 800.553.3199

EuroSpec Architectural Hardware
Fixtures—Door handles, hinges, security tools.
Web: www.eurospec.co.uk
Phone: +44 0.1254.274100

Fagan's Forge
Early American hardware—Supplier of hand-forged Early American door hardware and shutter hinges.
Web: www.fagansforge.com
Phone: 888.963.0130

Franchi Locks and Tools UK
Door furniture and accessories—Handles and locks: available in brass, chrome, bronze, or stainless steel; either polished or satin finishes.
Web: www.franchi.co.uk/door_furn.html
Phone: +44 0.870.60708090

Frank Allart
Home furnishings—Materials used: brass, aluminum, zinc, and bronze; products used in hotels, offices, schools, public buildings, royal palaces, and private houses.
Web: www.allart.co.uk
Phone: +44 (0)121.4106000

Ginger
Bathroom—Bath accessories.
Web: www.gingerco.com

Guerin, P. E.
Hardware—Manufacturer of hardware and accessories for doors, furniture, and baths.
Web: www.peguerin.com
Phone: 212.243.5270

Gulf Coast Shutter, Inc.
Shutters—Manufacturer of rolling, accordion, Bahama and Colonial shutters: storm screens and panels; awnings and hardware.
Web: www.westcoastshutters.com
Phone: 727.894.0044

Hand-Forged Traditional Ironmongery
Iron fixtures—Hinges, door knockers, rose-head nails, doorknobs, cabinet hooks, knobs, window fixtures, nails, studs.
Web: www.handforged.co.uk
Phone: +44 0.1584.876768

Hiles Plating Co.
Antique hardware—Restoration of antique hardware: custom finishes on new hardware; metal polishing and replating.
Web: www.hilesplating.com
Phone: 866.505.4460

The Home Depot
Home hardware—Appliances, electronics, flooring, furniture, garden plants, hand tools, heating and cooling, home decor, kitchen and bath, lighting and fans, outdoor, paint, plumbing, power tools, storage and organization, tool and truck rentals, workshop classes.
Web: www.homedepot.com
Phone: 800.553.3199

Hoppe
Locks—Door handles, window handles, door locks, window locks: many different styles of door handles as well as locks.
Web: www.us.hoppe.com
Phone: 888.485.4885

Horton Brasses
Reproduction hardware—More than 1,000 pieces of reproduction cabinet hardware
Web: www.horton-brasses.com
Phone: 800.754.9127

House of Antique Hardware
Antique hardware—Supplier of hardware: doors, hinges and more; rare and ornate hardware; antique (1860s–1930s).
Web: www.houseofantiquehardware.com
Phone: 888.223.2545

H.T. Sales Co., Inc.
Hardware and consulting—Distributor of door and window hardware: commercial washroom specialties; professional hardware consultants and specification writers on staff.
Web: www.htsalescompany.com
Phone New York City: 212.265.0747
Phone: 877.4273.9273 (877-HARDWARE)

ICI Paints
High-quality paints and coating available worldwide.
Web: www.icipaints.com

James Peters & Son, Inc.
Shutter hardware—Supplier of shutter hinges, dogs (holdbacks), bolts, and ring pulls.
Web: www.jamespetersandson.com
Phone: 215.739.9500

Kingsland Co. Shutters
Exterior shutters—Manufacturer of exterior shutters in Honduras mahogany: louvered, raised paneled, cutouts, and reproductions; mortise and tenon construction; copper caps, fixed control rods, and hardware.
Web: www.kingsland-shutters.com
Phone: 860.542.6981

Knob Deco
Decorative hardware—Doorknobs, handles, bathroom pulls, storage units in many unique designs.
Web: www.knobdeco.com
Phone: 888.566.2748

Kwikset
Door hardware—Locks, door handles, deadbolts, levers, knobs, specialty products.
Web: www.kwikset.com
Phone: 800.327.LOCK

LB Brass
Purveyor of fine quality European hardware.
Web: www.lbbrass.com
Phone: 718.786.8090

Liz's Antique Hardware
Home fixtures—bathroom, kitchen, door, window: styles are antique, contemporary, reproductions, and exclusive.
Web: www.lahardware.com
Phone: 323.939.4403

Lowe's
Home improvement store—Appliances, accessories, kitchens, dishwashers, lumber, showers, baths, grills, fencing, faucets, fixtures, lighting, outdoor equipment, insulation, doors, windows, gutters, plumbing, roofing, siding.
Web: www.lowes.com
Phone: 800.445.6937

Maguire Iron Corp.
Door and window hardware—Importer of traditional house hardware: door, window, cabinet, shutter, and gate hardware; more than 21,000 items.
Web: www.maguireironcorporation.com
Phone: 510.234.7569

Menards
Home improvement center—door, window and cabinet hardware.
Web: www.menards.com
Phone: 800.871.2800

Mitchell, D. C.
Handcast door hardware—Manufacturer of authentic reproductions of period door and shutter hardware.
Web: www.dcmitchell.org
Phone: 302.998.1181

Nanz Custom Hardware, Inc.
High-end period hardware—Manufacturer and supplier of door hardware: nineteenth-century, European, Modern, and Art Deco styles.
Web: www.nanz.com
Phone: 212.367.7000

Notting Hill Decorative Hardware
Pewter and bronze hardware—Supplier of decorative pulls, knobs, furniture, and cabinetry hardware: Victorian, Art Nouveau, and Art Deco.
Web: www.nottinghill-usa.com
Phone: 262.248.8890

Old Rose Company
Rosettes—Specializing in reproduction rosettes.
Web: www.oldrosehardware.com

Old Smithy Shop
Custom-forged iron hardware and more—Manufacturer of Early American–style forged hardware, for doors, windows, and shutters; forged or painted finishes; consultations.
Web: www.oldsmithyshop.com
Phone: 603.672.4113

Olivari
Doorknobs—Many doorknob styles to match your own.
Web: www.olivari.it/uk/produzione.html
Phone: +39 0.322.835080

Patten Design
Hardware, doors, and stairs—Manufacturer of cast-bronze hardware and hand-wrought iron doors, gates, staircases, lighting, and more.
Web: www.pattendesign.com
Phone: 714.894.0131

Phelps Company
Traditional door and window hardware—Manufacturer of door and window hardware: pulleys, weights, and more; manufactured to precision specs.
Web: www.phelpscompany.com
Phone: 802.257.4314

Rejuvenation
Period lighting—Lights, shades, door handles, locks, bath, window hardware, medicine cabinets, porch hardware, registers, drapery hardware, hooks, brackets, pulls.
Web: www.rejuvenation.com
Phone: 888.401.1900

Restoration Hardware
Home goods—Furniture, lighting, bedding, bath, windows and floors, hardware, utility and cleaning, accessories, gifts.
Web: www.restorationhardware.com
Phone: 800.762.1005

Reveal Designs
Hardware—Contemporary hardware designed by James Cutler.
Web: www.reveal-designs.com
Phone: 914.220.0277

Re-View
Window Restoration—Restorer of historic windows: wood and metal windows; replication, refurbishment, hardware restoration, and more.
Web: www.re-view.biz
Phone: 816.741.2876

Wm. J. Rigby
New old hardware—Unused architectural hardware dating from 1860 to 1960 that's never been used.
Web: www.wmjrigby.com
Phone: 607.547.1900

Rockler
Hardware tools—Furniture hardware, kitchen, entertainment center, home office, library hardware.
Web: www.rockler.com
Phone: 800.279.4441

Rocky Mountain Hardware
Bronze hardware—Door sets, hinges, door accessories, cabinet hardware, home accessories, kitchen and bath, sinks and faucets, window, tile, custom.
Web: www.rockymountainhardware.com
Phone: 888.788.2013

Restoration Resources
Salvage—one of New England's largest collections of antique salvage hardware.
Email: members.aol.com/wcrres
Phone: 617.542.3033

Samuel Heath
Bathroom accessories—Shower taps, brassware, hardware, doors furniture, ventilators, pull handles, suites; since 1820.
Web: www.Samuel-heath.com
Phone: +44 0.121.7722303

Schlage
Security fixtures—Locks, security, door handles, software.
Web: www.schlage.com
Phone: 800.805.9837

Stone River Bronze
Bronze accessories—Doorknobs, locks for doors and windows, cabinet covers, bath.
Web: www.stoneriverbronze.com
Phone: 435.755.8110

Sun Valley Bronze
Bronze hardware—Sun Valley Bronze offers a complete line of hand-crafted and hand-finished solid bronze door, kitchen, bath, and cabinet hardware.
Web: www.svbronze.com
Phone: 866.788.3631

Timberlane Woodcrafters
Shutter hardware—Maker of top quality shutters and shutter hardware.
Web: www.timberlaneshutters.com
Phone: 800.250.2221

Turnstyle Designs
Bath and door hardware: composites include glass, brass, pewter and wood; all fittings hand-crafted; lock fits, doorknobs, handles, window fittings.
Web: www.turnstyle-designs.com/home-prods.html
Phone: +44 0.1271.325325

Valli &Valli
Handles—High-quality door cabinet and sink hardware and fixtures from Italy.
Web: www.valliovalli.com
Phone: +39.0362982274

Van Dyke's Restorers
Reproduction hardware—Supplier of hardware, lighting, and antique furniture
Web: www.vandykes.com
Phone: 800.787.3355

Watercourt Traditional Ironmongery
Locks—Door fixtures, latches, handles, locks, fireplace fixtures.
Web: www.watercourt.co.uk
Phone: +44 0.1439.770323

Web Wilson/Old Rose Company
The Web source and online auction house for antique hardware.
Web: www.webwilson.com
Phone: 800.508.0022

Weiser Lock
Door locks, door handles—stylish, high-security locks for your home.
Web: www.weiserlock.com
Phone: 800.677.LOCK

Whitechapel Ltd.
Antique hardware—Furniture, cabinets, bed hardware, brackets, door bolts, stops, fasteners, hasps, hinges, hooks, key blanks, window hardware, door and cabinet locks, handles.
Web: www.whitechapel-ltd.com
Phone: 800.468.5534

Yale
Locks—Doorknobs, door handles, door locks, deadbolts, handle sets, levers.
Web: www.yalelock.com
Phone: 800.542.7562

Directory of Designers

Cover images: Bottom, clockwise: Gil Schafer, Architect; E. R. Butler Hardware, **top left**; Gil Schafer Architect, Pottery Barn Hardware, **top right**; Sandra Vitzthum, architect, Lucien Avery, blacksmith, **bottom left**; John B. Murray Architect, blacksmith, William Senseney, **bottom right**.

John Colamarino, Architect
Phone: 561.395.1787
p. 138

Dalia Kitchen Design
Mickey Green
Web: www.daliakitchendesign.com
Hardware shown exclusive to the Mark Wilkinson Cabinet Company
Web: www.mwf.com
p. 90

Mick DeGiulio
DeGiulio Kitchen & Bath
Web: www.degiulio.com
p. 94

Connie Driscoll
Phone: 508.228.8703
p. 142

Elliott Elliott Norelius Architecture
Web: www.elliottelliottnorelius.com
p. 106

Curtis Gelotte, Architect
Web: www.gelotte.com
p. 88

Garrison Hullinger
p. 126

Liza Kerrigan
Phone: 626.355.0027
p 84; 86

Morse Construction
Architect: Mark Wagner
Phone: 617.661.7175
Web: www.morseconstructions.com
p. 140

John B. Murray, Architect
Web: www.jbmmarchitect.com
p. 80; 152; 154

Frank Roop Design & Interiors
Web: www.frankroop.com
p. 92

Peter Rose, Architect
The Rose & Guggenheimer Studio
Web: www.roseguggenheimer.com
p. 136

Gil Schafer, Architect
p. 82; 156

Shope Reno Wharton Architecture
Web: www.shoperenowharton.com
p. 160

Dale Stewart, Architect
Core Architectural Design
www.coredc.com
p. 128; 158

Sandra Vitzthum, Architect
Web: www.sandravitzthum.com
p. 110; 116; 132; 134; 150

Eric Watson, Architect
Web: www.ericwatson.com
p. 162

Greg Wiedemann, Architect
Web: www.wiedemannarchitects.com
p. 120

Acknowledgments

About the Author

Putting a book together is a lot different than putting a magazine together—I think I'll definitely keep my day job! I would like to thank editor Candice Janco and project manager Betsy Gammons for their patience and encouragement during this process. I would also like to thank my former editors and mentors Gordon Bock, Barbara Tapp, Kathleen Fisher, and Paul Kitzke for helping me sharpen my skills as a writer and editor. Many, many thanks to the hardware companies that helped us put this book together including, E. R. Butler & Co., Crown City Hardware, Rejuvenation, Horton Brasses, Ball and Ball, Van Dyke's Restorers, Valli and Valli, Nanz, Liz's Antique Hardware, Gerber Hinge, Atlas Homewares, Reveal Designs, Rocky Mountain Hardware, Sun Valley Bronze, Acorn, Ginger, Craftman Homes Connection, and Craftsmen Hardware.

A special thanks to Baldwin Hardware, Timberlane Shutters, and Rockler Hardware for providing hardware for the installation steps as well as technical assistance. Thank you to Ball and Ball Hardware for sharing its extensive glossary of hardware terms. Thank you to Bill Raymer and Walter Santory at Restoration Resources in Boston for supplying antique hardware and imparting their extensive knowledge on the subject.

A very special thank you to my parents, Frank and Pat Downey, who always believed their kids could do anything they put their minds to.

While studying English literature at four schools around the country, Nancy E. Berry got a firsthand appreciation of America's vernacular architecture and the design details that make each regional style unique. Having lived in New England, on the West Coast, the Mid-Atlantic, and the Deep South, she combines her passions for writing and house design. She has been reporting on the subject of interior design and architecture for the past fifteen years as a staff editor for magazines such as *Atlanta Homes and Lifestyles*, *Cape Cod Home*, and *Old-House Journal*. Today, she is the editor of *Old-House Journal's* sister publication, *New Old House*. She currently lives on Cape Cod, where she is in search of antique Victorian hardware for her 1870 Queen Anne home.

Photographer Credits

Courtesy of Acorn Manufacturing Co., Inc., 21 (top); 57 (top);
104; 112; 116; 120 (bottom); 150 (middle); 154
Courtesy of Atlas Homewares, 92 (top); 118
Courtesy of Baldwin Hardware Corp., 16; 18; 56; 57 (third);
102 (bottom); 106; 108 (bottom); 138; 140 (bottom);
160; 162 (top)
Courtesy of Craftsmen Hardware Company, Ltd., 128;
158 (top, third & bottom)
Creative Publishing international, 7; 17; 21 (bottom);
24 (bottom); 25 (bottom); 58; 59; 60; 64; 65; 67; 68; 71; 73;
74; 75; 76; 82; 84; 86; 88; 92 (bottom); 100 (bottom); 108
(top & middle); 120 (top & middle); 122; 126 (middle &
bottom); 133; 134; 136 (top); 140 (top); 144; 146; 152;
156; 158 (second)
Guillaume DeLaubier, 13
Courtesy of Design Within Reach, 48
Courtesy of Ginger, 102 (top)
John Granen, 89
Steve Gross and Susan Daley, 105
Reto Guntli/www.zapaimages.com, 98; 113
Courtesy of Horton Brasses, Inc., 110
Courtesy of ICI Paints, maker of the Glidden Brand, 70; 79
Eric Johnson, 121; 129
Douglas Keister/www.keisterphoto.com, 41; 43
Courtesy of Laura Ashley Ltd./www.lauraashley.com, 115
Courtesy of Mackenzie-Childs, 124
Shelley Metcalf, 6; 33; 69
Michael Moran/Core Architectural Design, 4 (top); 159

Courtesy of Myson, 100 (top)
Don Pearse Photographers, Inc., 23
Pizzi + Thompson, 127
Courtesy of Rejuvenation, 12; 26 (right); 28 (middle & bottom);
126 (top)
Courtesy of Reveal Designs, LLC, 50; 51; 136 (bottom)
Courtesy of Rocky Mountain Hardware, 55; 98
Paul Rocheleau, 35 (top); 37
Eric Roth/www.ericrothphoto.com, 4 (bottom, right); 39; 90; 91;
93; 95; 111; 125; 141; 142; 143
Durston Saylor/John B. Murray, Architect, LLC, 81
Richard Sexton/www.richardsextonstudio.com, 163
Agi Simoes/www.zapaimages.com, 123; 145
Courtesy of Stone River Bronze, (second & bottom)
Robin Stubbert, 29; 31; 109; 131; 135
Linda Svendsen, 11; 45; 47
Courtesy of Timberlane Woodcrafters, 4 (bottom, left);
35 (bottom); 77; 162 (bottom)
Courtesy of Valli + Valli, 94
Brian Vanden Brink, 119
Brian Vanden Brink/John Colamarino, Architect, 139
Brian Vanden Brink/Elliott Elliott Norelius Architecture, 107
Brian Vanden Brink/Morningstar Marble & Granite, 103
Brian Vanden Brink/Peter Rose, Architect, 137
Brian Vanden Brink/Scholz & Barclay Architects, 147
Brian Vanden Brink/Scogin, Elam & Bray, Architects, 97
Brian Vanden Brink/ Shope, Reno, & Wharton Architecture, 161
Courtesy of Van Dyke's Restorers, 57 (fourth)
Jonathan Wallen, 9; 19; 49; 53; 83; 101; 153; 155; 157
Jim Westphalen, 133
Charles White, 63; 85; 87
Nancy Easter White, 27
Dominic Whiting/Elizabeth Whiting &
Associates/www.ewastock.com, 149
Elizabeth Whiting & Associates/www.ewastock.com, 21 (middle)
James Yochum, 117; 150 (top & bottom); 151